Flip Your Way
to Fabulous Quilts

Take Folded Corners to New Heights

Donna Lynn Thomas

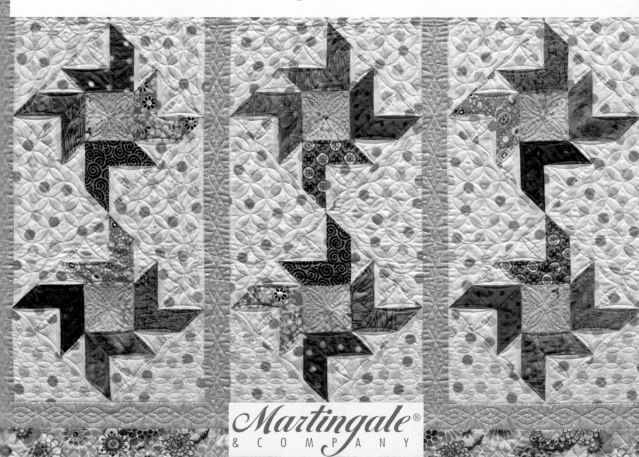

Martingale®
& COMPANY

Flip Your Way to Fabulous Quilts:
Take Folded Corners to New Heights
© 2011 by Donna Lynn Thomas

That Patchwork Place® is an imprint of
Martingale & Company®.

Martingale & Company
19021 120th Ave. NE, Suite 102
Bothell, WA 98011-9511
www.martingale-pub.com

Credits

President & CEO: Tom Wierzbicki
Editorial Director: Mary V. Green
Managing Editor: Tina Cook
Developmental Editor: Karen Costello Soltys
Design Director: Stan Green
Technical Editor: Laurie Baker
Copy Editor: Melissa Bryan
Production Manager: Regina Girard
Illustrator: Robin Strobel
Cover & Text Designer: Stan Green
Photographer: Brent Kane

Printed in China
16 15 14 13 12 11   8 7 6 5 4 3 2

**Library of Congress Cataloging-in-Publication Data
is available upon request.**

ISBN: 978-1-60468-023-2

Mission Statement

Dedicated to providing quality products and service to inspire creativity.

Dedication

To my Prairie Chick quilting friend Linda Harker, who passed away June 16, 2010, at the too-young age of 55. Despite a three-and-a-half-year battle with a ferocious cancer, she still found time to test and make samples for this book. She was an inspiration to all who knew her for her sense of humor until the end, her fierce and determined fight, her upbeat approach to everything she encountered in life, and her beautiful quilts. Quilting saw her through her troubles just like it does for so many of us.

It's hard to believe you're gone so soon, but Linda, this one's for you!

Instructions for the quilt that inspired Linda's quilts are on page 54.

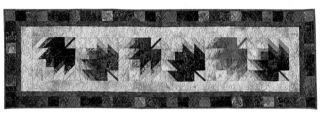

My Favorite Colors by Linda Harker, 18½" x 58½"; machine quilted by Denise Mariano. These richly vibrant leaves were meant for Linda's cheerful, brightly colored dining room.

Linda's Finale by Linda Harker, 39½" x 39½"; machine quilted by Denise Mariano. Linda loved bright, beautiful quilts, and she sprinkled happy blues and greens across this table topper with her usual abandon—you can't help but smile.

Acknowledgments

Big thanks to the design, editorial, and support staffs at Martingale & Company, who consistently make working with them a breeze. A special thanks is due to my tech editor, Laurie Baker; editors always make the authors look better than we are. Their patience is abundant.

Many thanks to all the wonderful quilters who sew, test, bind, quilt, and do all sorts of creative, supportive things that make a book possible. You are my quilting fairy heroes!

To Freda Smith, Karen Kielmeyer, Pam Goggans, Marilyn Gore, Darlene Szabo, Sandy Gore, Kelly Ashton, Kim Pope, Denise Mariano, and Shirley Jenkins for the beautiful quilting they do. A quilt is not a quilt until it's quilted.

To Linda Harker, Gabriel Pursell, Pam Goggans, Katharine Brigham, Beth Woods, Shirley "Kiwi" Brown, Kay Harman, Linda Kittle, Ysleta Meek, Kim Pope, Karen Kielmeyer, Barbara Eikmeier, Jennie Wehrenberg, Toni Fenton, and Alice Zeman for testing patterns and/or making samples for the book.

To Cathy Reitan and Becky Robertson for help with binding, and to debi Schrader for help with binding and also for proofreading the manuscript that one last time.

To my new quilting daughter-in-law, Katie Thomas, for her tremendous help in all manner of details and admini-trivia during the crunch time right before the manuscript and quilts were sent off!

Thank you, one and all!

Contents

Introduction

I've always been intrigued by the effects one can achieve using several fabrics in a pieced unit to create a striped pattern. In the 1990s I wrote two books, *Stripples* and *Stripples Strikes Again!*, that explored the use of squares, rectangles, and triangles cut from pieced strips. I developed intricate bias-strip units from which to cut out shapes, along with a special ruler, the Bias Stripper, for cutting the bias strips to specific sizes. The technique worked beautifully but was difficult for others to replicate. Quilters didn't want to tackle designing those strip units alone, and I can't say I blame them—you have to be a math nut like me to want to do it.

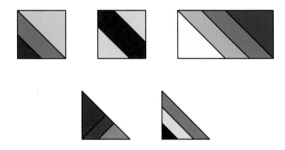

The possibilities for fun with these shapes continued to intrigue me over the years, but I knew I needed to develop a simple, easy-to-do method for achieving the striped effect. You might think that a string-piecing technique would do the trick, but the stripes in a string-pieced unit are too irregular. I needed to be able to control the measurements of the stripes precisely so that they could be matched with other patches, squares, and units to create specific designs.

I know from experience that if I let something stew in the back of my mind, the answer often shows itself with time. I was not disappointed. Driving home from teaching a workshop one day, I was playing around with ideas in my mind yet again and—bam! There it was in full form! I pulled over to the side of the road and wrote down my thoughts. The next day I set aside time to implement the concept on the most difficult block I could imagine for this process, and it worked perfectly! The bonus was that the technique was as simple as can be for anyone to use and was based on a familiar technique—folded corners.

If you've been quilting for a few years you've probably run across the simple concept of folded corners: sew a smaller square to the corner of a larger square or rectangle, and then fold it over to make a triangle on the corner. By expanding on that familiar technique, I was able to get exactly the results I wanted. Now I could start designing with all those glorious striped units again using a process anyone could repeat. What fun!

If you're not familiar with the folded-corners technique or you simply need a refresher, I've covered the basics in "Simple Folded Corners" on page 16. "Applying the Concept" on page 18 expands the technique to teach you how to create the striped squares, rectangles, and triangles needed to make the quilts in this book. Be sure to read these sections carefully before making a quilt. There are a lot of tips and hints on how to be successful using this exciting new concept.

Once you read and understand the technique, browse through the 13 quilt projects, which are divided into three skill sections. The first section, "Try Me Quilts," contains projects that use the most basic skills. I encourage you to try at least a block or two from one of these projects to make sure you understand the folded-corners process before proceeding with the other sections. Start with these quilts if you're a relative newcomer to quiltmaking but confident in your ability to cut and sew accurately.

The second section, "Grow with Me Quilts," progresses into units with more stripes. These patterns are geared for those of intermediate skills or confident beginners who have been successful with a block or project from the first section.

"Master Me Quilts" are the more challenging projects, either in design or in demand for precision skills. The skills aren't any different from those involved in the other quilts, but there may be more pieces in each block, narrower stripes, or more stripes, all of which require precision to accomplish successfully. Be sure of your ability to cut and sew accurately before starting a quilt from this section. Practice on an easier project if necessary to improve your technique.

You'll find a wide assortment of quilt patterns as well as alternate color options for some of the patterns given. The idea is to give you permission to stray from the color choices I've made! As a bonus, I've also included one final block and quilt idea that makes use of the leftover triangles trimmed away (I call them "trim-aways") from your quilts.

I hope you enjoy working with this new idea and find all kinds of possibilities and uses for it in your own quilts. Enjoy!

Basic Quiltmaking Techniques

To make the quilts in this book, you need only basic rotary-cutting and machine-piecing supplies and skills. Beyond that, however, I have provided a few tips and tricks that enhance the process of making striped squares, rectangles, and triangles.

Tools and Supplies

You'll want the following basic tools and supplies on hand.

- Sewing machine
- 80/12 Sharp sewing-machine needles
- Rotary-cutting mat, cutter, and rulers (including the Bias Square ruler, which is optional but useful for the technique explained in "Add-an-Inch Bias Squares" on page 11)
- Good pair of sharp fabric shears and a pair of small thread clips

- Seam ripper
- Silk pins
- Chalk marking pencils
- Fine-line mechanical pencil
- Sandpaper board (or make your own by covering a self-adhesive needlework mounting board with super-fine sandpaper)

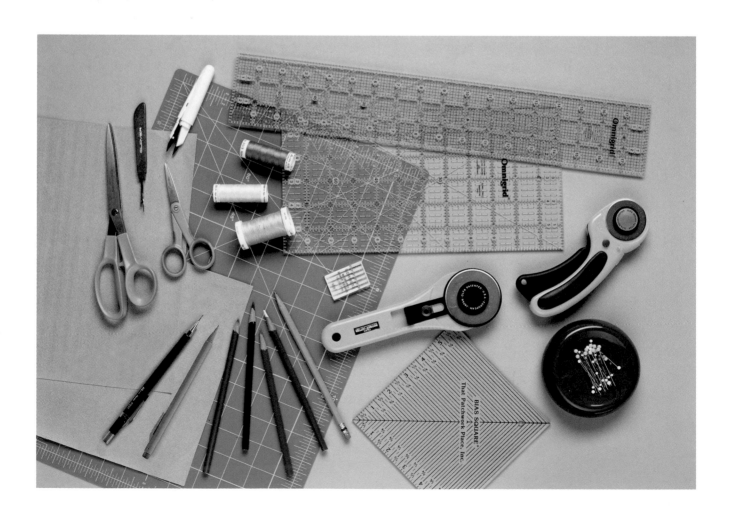

Seam Allowance

Accuracy is important in every aspect of quiltmaking. Because precise seam-allowance dimensions are included in the pieces you cut, it is imperative that you sew using an accurate ¼" seam allowance. If your seam allowance is too wide or too narrow, the small errors on each seam snowball into a frustrating, inaccurate end result. Ideally, your seams and intersections should fall together into a perfect match.

Conduct a test on your machine to determine the accuracy of your ¼" seam guide and your ability to use it correctly.

1. Cut three 1½" x 3" strips of fabric. Check the 1½" width of each strip for accuracy.

2. Sew the strips together side by side along the long edges. Align the raw edges carefully, and sew slowly and accurately by using the machine's ¼" seam guide.

3. Press the two seam allowances away from the center strip. The center strip should measure exactly 1" from seam to seam.

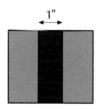

If the center strip is off by just a thread or two, check your sewing habits first.

- Were the raw edges aligned and did you keep them that way while stitching?

- Did you sew too fast to properly control the edges while stitching?

- Is your stitching line straight?

- Were the strips cut exactly 1½" wide, or were they just kind of close?

Errors in these little details are often the source of inaccurate seams. The solution is to slow down. Take the time to be careful and accurate when cutting and sewing.

Your machine could also be the problem.

- Does your presser foot hold the fabric layers snug enough to keep them aligned?

- Do the feed dogs feed fabric through without shifting layers?

If the machine does not operate properly, get it repaired. The reduction in frustration and seam ripping more than compensates for the effort.

If, despite careful stitching, the center strip still does not measure exactly 1" wide, check the seam guide.

1. Cut a 2" x 6" piece of ¼" graph paper. Put the paper under the presser foot and lower the needle into the paper, just barely to the right of the first ¼" grid line, so that the needle is included in the dimension of the seam allowance. Otherwise, the stitching will decrease the size of the finished area by a needle's width on each seam you sew.

2. Adjust the paper so it runs straight forward from the needle, angling neither to the left nor to the right. Lower the presser foot to hold the paper in place. Tape the left edge of the paper down so it won't slip.

3. Check the machine's ¼" guide against the edge of the graph paper. If the guide is the edge of the presser foot, the edge should run along the edge of the graph paper. If the guide is an etched line on the throat plate, the same should be true.

If the edge of the presser foot or etched line does not run along the edge of the graph paper, you need to make a new guide. Place a piece of masking tape or self-stick foam along the edge of the graph paper as shown. Make sure it is in front of and out of the way of the feed dogs.

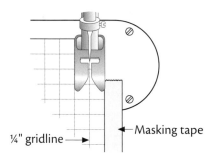

¼" gridline ⟶   ⟵ Masking tape

Put masking tape in front of
needle along edge of graph paper.

4. Do another strip test to check this new guide. Adjust the tape guide as necessary until you can conduct strip tests accurately several times in a row. If you're using masking tape, build up the guide with several layers of tape to create a ridge that will help you guide the fabric.

Pressing

A properly pressed seam allowance is cleanly and crisply pressed to one side, without any pleats, distortions, or puckers on the right side. Here are a few tips that will help you.

Press, don't iron, your seams. Ironing is an aggressive, back-and-forth motion that can easily pull and distort the bias grain or seams in your piecing. Pressing is the gentle lowering, pressing, and lifting of the iron along the straight grain of a seam. Let the heat do the work.

Always press the seam line flat after sewing but before turning. This is called setting the thread. Setting the thread relaxes the thread, eases out any puckers, smooths out any minor fullness you may

have eased in as you stitched, and helps the thread sink into the weave of the fabric, making for a nice, smooth turn.

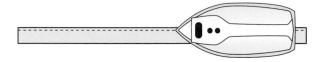

Use a dry iron on the cotton setting. Steam distorts. If it's necessary to put a stronger crease in a seam, lightly mist the seam with a spray bottle or starch alternative after it's pressed. Then, without any back-and-forth motion, press the seam dry to form a nice crease.

Position the unit to be pressed on your ironing surface so that the fabric you'll be pressing the seam allowances toward is on top. Place the open edges of the fabric pieces toward you and the stitched seam away from you. Use the tip of the iron to carefully open the unit, exposing the right side, and then gently press the top fabric over the seam allowance. Always move the iron in the direction of the straight grain of the fabric. Pressing along the bias will stretch your pieces.

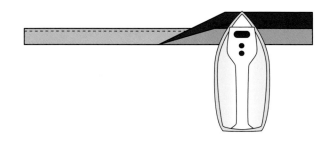

To correct mistakes in pressing, return the unit to its original unpressed position and press the seam flat to remove the crease. A particularly crisp seam may need a spritz of water to relax the crease. Once you've removed the original crease, press the seam allowances in the new direction.

PRESS AS DIRECTED

Pressing directions have been determined for you in all the projects in this book and are indicated by small arrows in the diagrams. Please pay attention to them and press as directed. The goal of these directions is to provide you with seam allowances that oppose each other whenever possible, creating intersections that meet and lie flat, and helping you avoid a great deal of frustration when sewing.

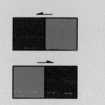

Add-an-Inch Bias Squares

Bias squares (pieced squares) are traditionally composed of two half-square triangles sewn together along their long bias edges. Normally, to make bias squares, we cut half-square triangles from squares that are ⅞" larger than the desired finished size of the short edge of the triangle. Unfortunately, once sewn together, the resulting bias squares are often distorted or inaccurate in size.

Finished size of pieced unit

With add-an-inch bias squares, you instead cut and sew slightly oversized triangles to make slightly oversized bias squares, and then trim the bias squares to the required size. The result is perfectly sized bias squares every time with a minimum of effort.

To begin, cut half-square triangles from squares that are 1" larger than the finished size,

instead of the more precise ⅞". Hence the name, "add-an-inch bias squares." For example, to make two bias squares that will finish to 2":

1. Choose two prints for the bias squares and cut a 3" square from each print (1" larger than the desired 2" finished size).

2. Place the two squares right sides together.

3. Cut the pair of squares in half diagonally to make two pairs of half-square triangles.

4. Sew each pair of triangles on their bias edges using ¼" seam allowances. Press carefully, keeping the iron on the straight grain so as not to distort or stretch the seam.

5. Trim each bias square to 2½" (trim size − finished size + ½") using the Bias Square ruler. Put the diagonal line of the ruler on the seam of the bias square when you trim each of the four sides.

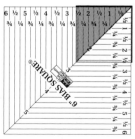

Place diagonal line of ruler on seam line. Trim first two sides.

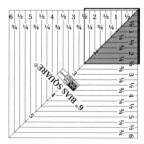

Align desired measurement on previously cut edge and diagonal line on seam. Trim remaining sides.

Completing Your Quilt

Once your blocks are done, you will be anxious to start adding borders and completing the top.

Please be sure to read this section as it includes information on my preferred methods for borders, backings, and binding. It's important for you to understand these methods in order to change them if you prefer a different approach. For instance, if you'd rather cut lengthwise border strips or make a wider binding, you'll need to adjust the fabric and cutting requirements accordingly.

Borders

The quilts in this book use either plain borders or pieced borders. Information for adding both types is given here.

Before adding borders, clean up loose threads or triangle tips from the edges of your quilt top. For a straight-set quilt there shouldn't be much else to do, but for a diagonally set quilt top, you will need to straighten the edges. This type of quilt is often made with oversized side and corner setting triangles that need to be trimmed to size. To do this, align the ¼" line of a large ruler with the block or sashing points on the sides of the quilt top, and trim the quilt edges to ¼" from these points. Use a large square ruler to trim both sides of a corner at the same time so that the corner will be square when the trimming is complete.

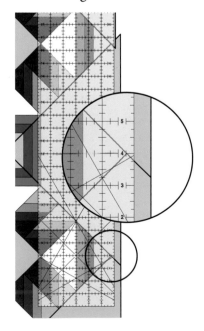

Plain Borders

Plain borders are unpieced plain strips of fabric added around the center design area of a quilt. They're similar to the matting that framers put around a painting or print. The quantity of borders, the colors you choose, and the variety of widths all enhance the center of the quilt.

There are several ways to measure, cut, and sew plain borders. The quilts in this book use my favorite, fabric-efficient method. One of the benefits of this method is that the seams are fairly obscure visually. If the seams line up perfectly in the middle of each border, your eye will pick out the symmetry and focus in on that quickly. Random seams, however, are more likely to go unnoticed. If you have a different favorite method, please be aware that you may need to recalculate fabric and cutting requirements for your border prints.

1. I prefer to cut strips on the crosswise grain of fabric (selvage to selvage). Cut strips the desired finished border width plus ½" for seam allowances. Determine how many strips you need by measuring the four sides of your quilt and adding these numbers together. Add four times the border width to this number and divide by 40 to determine how many strips to cut.

2. Once you've cut your strips, sew them together end to end into one continuous strip using simple, straight ¼" seam allowances. Some people like to use diagonal seams to join the strips, but I don't see any great benefit to it and a bit of fabric goes to waste. In fact, I suspect the bias seam is more liable to stretch than a

straight-grain seam. There are times, though, when the print of a fabric will hide a diagonal seam better than a straight seam. In that case, I will use a diagonal seam. Design trumps all.

3. Once the strips are sewn together, measure the length of your completed quilt top through the center. Cut two strips from your long border strip to fit this dimension, *regardless of where the seams will fall on the side of the quilt.* Sew these two strips to the sides of the quilt, easing to fit a bit if necessary.

4. Press the seam allowances away from the center of the quilt. By cutting the borders to the center length, you'll bring in the sides of the quilt to be square with the center, if they aren't already. Large discrepancies in the measurements between center and sides cannot be eased in and must be addressed. This may require some repair work on the center of the quilt to bring it more in line with its correct size.

5. Now measure the center width of the quilt top, including the side borders. Cut two strips from the remainder of the border strip to this dimension and sew them to the top and bottom of the quilt, easing in a bit if necessary. Press the seam allowances away from the center of the quilt unless otherwise instructed.

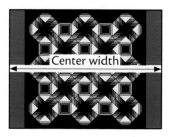

SEAMS ON THE EDGE

There may be an occasion when a border seam will fall just short of the edge of the quilt side if you cut it straight from the long piece. In that case, reposition and cut the strip so that the seam falls well within the side boundaries of the quilt.

6. Repeat steps 1–5 to add any remaining plain borders to the quilt top.

Pieced Borders

It's easiest to sew pieced borders to quilt tops that are the proper size. If the measurements of the quilt center are considerably different from what they should be, figure out what's wrong and take the steps to correct it before attaching the pieced border. If the quilt top is wildly off-size, it may be necessary to recalculate the border piecing or drop it entirely. Small discrepancies can usually be handled, though.

1. Measure the center length of the quilt top. Measure the length of the pieced borders that will go on the sides of the quilt top. If they're equal, pin and sew the pieced borders to the sides of the quilt top, positioning and pinning any seams that need to be aligned with quilt-top seams. If there is a slight difference in the sizes of the borders and quilt sides, take in or let out a little from *several* seams on the pieced borders until they fit the dimensions of the quilt sides. Do not take in or let out only one seam or its difference in size will be very noticeable. A tiny adjustment in many seams will go unnoticed.

2. Follow the same procedure to measure the center width of the quilt, adjust the top and bottom pieced borders as needed, and sew the borders into place.

Quilt Backings

Most of the quilts in this book require a paneled backing unless you purchase super-wide backing fabric. To figure the yardage for a two-panel backing, measure the length of your quilt top, add 6" to 8" for margin, and double this amount. Divide this figure by 36" to determine the number of yards you need. Add 10% for shrinkage. To figure the yardage for a three-panel backing, measure the length of your quilt top, add 6" to 8" for margin, and triple the amount. Continue determining yardage as for a two-panel backing.

After washing the fabric, cut and sew it into a two- or three-panel backing as needed. Cut the backing 3" to 4" larger than the quilt top on all sides.

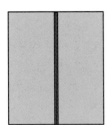

Two ways to piece paneled backings

Binding

The binding is the band of fabric sewn to the final edge of the quilt to finish it. I prefer to cut and sew crossgrain strips for a double-fold binding. To determine the number of strips needed, measure the four sides of your quilt top, add the numbers together plus 10" to 12" for turning and ending, and then divide the result by 40 (the useable width of the fabric).

Making Binding

1. Cut 2¼"-wide strips from selvage to selvage for standard ¼"-wide finished binding.

2. With right sides together, join the strips into one long piece of binding by stitching the ends together at right angles. Trim away excess fabric and press the seam allowances open. Use closely matching thread to avoid peekaboo stitches at the seams.

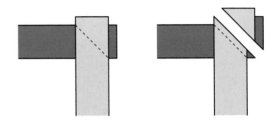

3. Fold the strip in half lengthwise, wrong sides together, and press. Cut one end of the strip at a 45° angle and press under the end ¼".

Fold line

Attaching Binding

1. Baste the three layers of the quilt securely at the outer edges if you have not already done so. Trim the batting and backing even with the quilt-top edges and corners.

2. In the center of one edge of the quilt, align the raw edges of the binding with the raw edge of the quilt top. Leaving about 6" free as a starting tail, sew the binding to the edge of the quilt with a ¼"-wide seam allowance. Use an even-feed presser foot on your sewing machine to better handle the thick layers smoothly. Stop

stitching ¼" from the corner of the first side. Backstitch and remove the quilt from the machine.

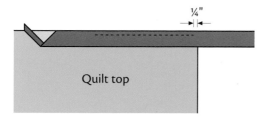

3. At the corner, flip the binding straight up from the corner so that it forms a continuous line with the adjacent side of the quilt top. Fold the binding straight down to lie on top of the next side. Pin the pleat in place. Starting at the edge, stitch the second side of the binding to the quilt, stopping ¼" from the next corner. Repeat for the remaining corners.

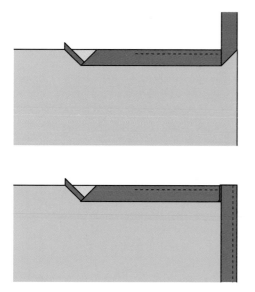

4. When you've turned the last corner and are nearing the point where you began, stop and overlap the binding ends by about 1". Cut away any excess binding, trimming the end

to a 45° angle. Tuck the end into the fold and finish the seam. Hand slipstitch the fold on the overlapped binding to close it.

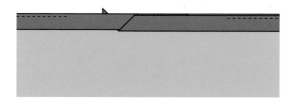

5. Turn the binding to the back of the quilt and slipstitch it to the backing to complete the binding—and your quilt!

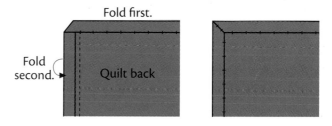

Labeling Your Quilt

Be sure to sign and date your quilt. Labels can be simple or elaborate. They can be handwritten, typed, or embroidered. Be sure to include the name of the quilt, your name, your city and state, the date, and the name of the recipient if it's a gift. Include interesting or important information about the quilt. Future generations will want to know more about the quilt than just who made it and when.

Simple Folded Corners

The basic idea of folded corners is to sew a square of fabric to the corner of a larger "parent" square, and then fold over the smaller square to duplicate a corner triangle.

Use the following simple step-by-step process to make all types of folded-corner units.

1. Determine the finished size of the corner triangle where it falls on the side of the main unit. Add ½" to this measurement and cut a square this size. In the example given, you would cut a 2½" square to sew onto the 4" finished parent square.

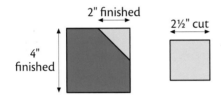

2. Draw a diagonal line on the wrong side of the smaller corner square. This line must be very fine and accurate, running exactly from corner to corner. To keep the fabric from shifting as you mark, place the square on a sandpaper board or super-fine sandpaper. To further reduce shifting, hold your pencil at a 45° angle so the point does not drag in the weave of the fabric. Carefully place the smaller square on the corner of the larger parent unit with right sides together. Sew on the marked line.

Draw line.   Stitch on line.

NO-MARK METHOD

Instead of drawing a pencil line, make a corner-sewing guide in front of your needle on the throat plate and work surface of your machine. This method doesn't really work well if your machine doesn't sit down into a table or have an attachable worktable to provide the space needed. There are several commercially sold angle-sewing guides designed for this technique, but you can make one for yourself using just masking tape.

Unthread your needle and lower it into the throat plate. Lay a ruler to the left of your needle running in a direct line forward from the needle. Place a crosswise ruler line on the front edge of the throat plate to help ensure the ruler is running straight in line from the needle and perpendicular to the front edge of the throat plate. You don't want your final guide to be skewed to the left or right. To make the guide, lay a piece of masking tape on the right edge of the ruler so it, too, is running in a direct line forward from the needle. Now when you sew, place the first corner to be sewn right up in front of the needle with the far corner aligned with the tape. Keep it aligned as you sew and your seam should run straight on the diagonal from corner to corner without the need for a drawn line.

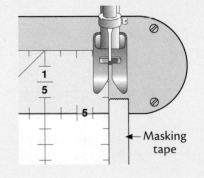

Masking tape

3. Press the small square back over the corner, right side facing up, and check it for accuracy. Be careful not to stretch it. It should lie exactly on the corner of the parent unit. If it doesn't, check the accuracy of the marked line or your sewing and adjust as needed. If the square comes up short of the corner, you may need to sew a thread's width closer to the corner of the unit. If the square is too big for the corner, check to make sure you're sewing exactly from corner to corner and your pieces are lined up properly. If there is consistent trouble, check the accuracy of the corner-square size, the parent-unit size, the drawn line, or your sewing to find and correct the source of the problem. Each seam must be accurate in order for your final unit to finish at the size it's meant to be.

Fold square over corner.

4. Trim away both extra layers of fabric under the top corner triangle ¼" from the stitching line.

With these basic instructions, you can use folded corners to make all the shapes shown here.

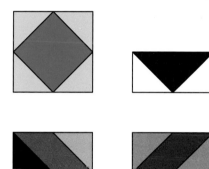

IMPROVE YOUR ACCURACY

Here are some additional tips to help ensure your success with the folded-corners technique.

- Use an open-toe presser foot so you can see to place the first corner precisely in front of the needle.
- Use a straight-stitch throat plate, if you have one, to keep corners from being sucked into the larger hole of a regular throat plate and mangled.
- Lift your presser foot slightly to place each piece under the foot. Running it under the lowered presser foot without lifting can misalign the top piece.
- Always sew with the corner to be trimmed away to the right of the needle. This is very important or you will often end up with folded corners that are too small.
- Some machines lose control of the far corners as they sew. If this is a problem, put a pin through the layers to the right of the far corner to keep the layers from shifting as you sew. Because the pin is positioned out of the way of the oncoming needle, it does not need to be removed to prevent needle breakage. You don't usually need a pin in the first corner since it goes directly under the presser foot.

Applying the Concept

Now that you're familiar with the most basic form of folded corners, we can expand into striped units. The "layers" are the stripes or gradations of color formed along the length of the rectangle, square, or triangle.

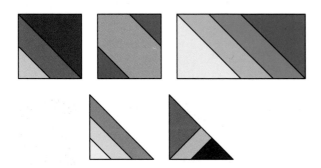

The stripes are created in the same fashion as basic folded corners: draw a 45° diagonal line, sew on the line, press, and trim the excess. And, of course, you may use a corner-sewing guide instead of drawing a line, just as with the basic method.

Striped Squares

Striped squares are basic folded corners, only the process is repeated one or more times in succession on one or more corners to create stripes.

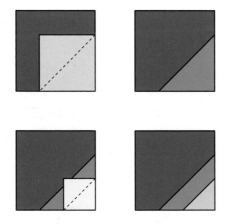

The stripes can be on one side of the square or on opposite sides, in the middle or at the corners, and there can be as many stripes as you wish of whatever widths you desire.

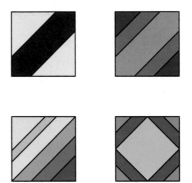

Striped squares start with a "parent" square onto which the smaller squares are sewn. This parent square can be a plain, unpieced square or it can be a pieced bias square, which provides a center diagonal seam.

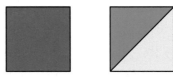

Determining Cut Sizes for Striped Squares

Determining the size to cut the parent square is simple. For a plain parent square, determine the finished size along the edge and add ½" for the cut size. To use a pieced bias square as the parent square, determine the finished size, and then add 1" and make a bias square following the instructions in "Add-an-Inch Bias Squares" on page 11. Trim the bias square to the finished size plus ½" for the seam allowance.

Determining the sizes of squares for the folded corners is equally simple. Just as with basic folded corners, determine the cut size by adding ½" to the finished distance from the corner to the far edge of the stripe.

In the example shown, assume a 4" finished-size striped square with two stripes that measure 1" on the edge of the square. The triangle on the inner corner measures 2". Because there is a diagonal seam that runs from corner to corner, start with a bias square as the parent square. Please note that the first stripe parallel to the diagonal seam is formed by the bias square itself after the subsequent fabrics are folded in place.

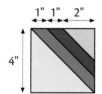

Finished measurements

- For the parent bias square, use 5" squares (1" larger than 4" finished size) to make a bias square as described in "Add-an-Inch Bias Squares," and trim it to 4½".

- For the 1" center stripe, cut a square that is 3½". This is the distance from the corner (2" + 1") plus ½" for seam allowance.

- For the small folded corner, cut a square that is 2½" (2" from corner + ½").

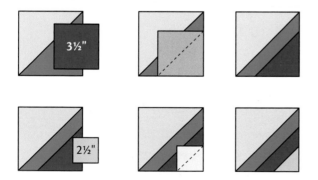

Striped Rectangles

Making striped rectangles is a bit different than making striped squares. Rather than sewing smaller squares to the corners of larger parent squares, we sew squares and shortened rectangles onto each other to form a striped rectangle.

THE RIGHT ANGLE

Striped rectangles have mirror images, so you must position and sew pieces in the correct direction in order to create the correct angle. When following project instructions, be careful to orient the rectangles exactly as shown in the illustrations.

---

1. Begin with the square that makes the first corner. If you're not using a corner-sewing guide, mark the diagonal line on the wrong side of the square in the same manner as for basic folded corners.

2. Place the square on the corner of the rectangle that makes the first stripe after the corner square as shown, right sides together. Check the orientation visually by folding over the square onto the corner where it will lie to make sure it forms the correct angle. Adjust the pieces if necessary, and then sew them together on the line.

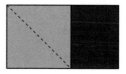

3. Check the accuracy of your seam and adjust if needed. Press the seam allowances in the desired direction. Trim away the excess, leaving a ¼" seam allowance.

4. Mark the diagonal on the wrong side of the rectangle that forms the next stripe in the sequence. Because marking corner to corner on a rectangle will not create the desired angle, you must mark using a ruler with a 45° line that ends on the corner of the ruler (the diagonal line of a Bias Square ruler works perfectly). Depending on the direction of the line, mark with the 45° line on either the short edge or the long edge of the rectangle.

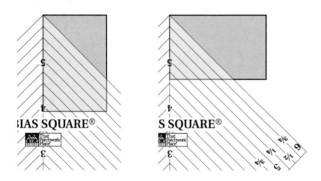

Note: If you're using a taped corner-sewing guide on your sewing machine, you'll need to make a pencil mark on the edge of the rectangle where it lies over the corner of the unit underneath. This mark is your guide to place on the corner-sewing guide as the pieces move toward the needle.

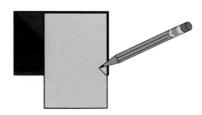

5. Position the marked rectangle on the previous rectangle, right sides together, so the edges are aligned with the correct corner. The remainder of the rectangle will extend above or below the base. Be careful to orient the diagonal line so that the rectangle will fold over into the correct position. Sew, press, and trim as usual.

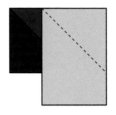 

RECTANGLE REMINDERS

To help me remember which way to orient the rectangles, I use two simple mantras: "Corner up, (rectangle) tail down" and "Corner down, tail up." In the first example here, the corner of the first rectangle is on the upper-right side, which means the rectangle for the next stripe is oriented on the first rectangle with the excess tail down. In the second, the reverse is true. In other words, the corner and the tail are never together on the same side.

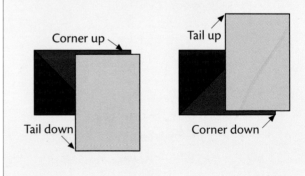

6. Continue adding rectangles one by one in the same fashion. Finish the unit by sewing the last corner square in place in the same way as any folded corner.

You can make many types of striped rectangles with this technique. Below are some examples of different ways to stripe rectangles. The only limit is your imagination.

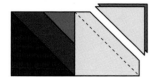

Determining Cut Sizes for Striped Rectangles

Unlike striped squares, there is no base unit upon which the striped rectangle originates. Striped rectangles are simply built in a linear fashion with squares and rectangles. As always, determining the cut sizes of the squares and rectangles that make up the striped rectangle is based on knowing the finished sizes.

STRAIGHT STRIPES

To avoid creating curved rainbows instead of striped rectangles, follow these tips.

If your seams aren't sewn precisely from the corner of the rectangle on top to the opposite diagonal corner of the unit on the bottom, or if the far corners slip off point consistently when sewing, the stripes will be bigger than they should be on one side. The end result, instead of a rectangle, is a curved rainbow—which, although pretty, unfortunately doesn't fit nicely with the other square pieces of your block. The solution is to be very careful when sewing and resort to a pin or two if necessary to hold everything in place while stitching.

If you sew too far to the left or right of the marked diagonal line when you're adding the rectangles for the stripes, your stripes will be either oversized or undersized, again resulting in rainbows or rectangles that are too large or too small. If you're using a corner-sewing guide, try slowing down when you sew, or switch to a drawn line for a while to see if that is more accurate for you.

Press on a gridded ironing-board cover or mat. Carefully nudge your corners into place, staying within the gridded boundaries of your rectangle at each stage of sewing. Be sure to use a dry iron. You can spray mist to create a crisp seam only after the seam is completely in place. Don't move the iron across the surface of the fabric when it's wet—only move the iron up and down.

When all else fails, go back and check your cutting. Are you cutting the right sizes? It's surprising how many times this is the culprit.

Let's look at this example of a 2" x 4" finished-size striped rectangle. Each of the stripes measures 1" on the edge of the rectangle. The corner triangles are 2". Corner triangles are always equal to the shortest edge of the finished rectangle.

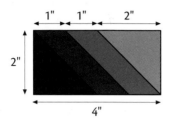

Finished measurements

The corner triangles on a striped rectangle are basic folded corners. As such, the squares cut for the corners measure the finished size of the short triangle edge plus ½" for seams. In this case, that is 2½". This is the same calculation used for basic folded corners, as well as striped squares.

As you can see from the striped rectangle construction process described previously, we make the stripes by folding rectangles onto the unit. Therefore, we need to figure both the short edge and the long edge of those rectangles.

- The short edge is equal to the short edge of the finished unit, which would be 2" in the example shown. Add ½" for seam allowances to determine the cut size (2½").

- Calculate the long edge of the rectangle by adding the finished size of the stripe on the edge (1" in this case) to the short edge of the finished unit (2" in this case). Add ½" for seam allowances to this measurement to determine the cut size (3½").

For this rectangle, each rectangle for making a 1" stripe will be cut 2½" x 3½".

Striped Triangles

There are three main categories of striped triangles made using the folded-corners concept: center-striped, side-striped, and simple-striped. The stripes in center-striped triangles run parallel to the longest edge of the triangle, whereas side-striped triangles feature stripes running parallel to one short side of the triangle. Simple-striped triangles do not run parallel to any edge of the triangle, but rather perpendicular to the long edge.

Center-striped   Side-striped   Simple-striped

Center-Striped Triangles

Think of a center-striped triangle as half of a striped square. We calculate sizes, cut, and sew in the same fashion as for striped squares. The only difference is that we fold smaller squares onto a base triangle instead of a base square. Depending on where the finished triangle is used and its grain-line needs, the base triangle will be either a half-square triangle (a square cut in half diagonally) or a quarter-square triangle (a square cut into quarters diagonally). To avoid stretching and distortion, always position the triangle so that the straight grain is on the outer edge of the block or quilt.

1. Begin by deciding on the desired finished size of the triangle along the short edge if it's to be a half-square triangle or along the long edge if it's to be a quarter-square triangle. If you need the straight grain on the short edge, cut half-square base triangles by adding ⅞" to the finished size of the short side. If you need the straight grain on the long edge, cut quarter-square triangles

by adding 1¼" to the finished size of the long edge.

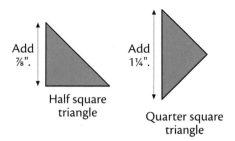

Add ⅞".
Half square triangle

Add 1¼".
Quarter square triangle

2. To determine the size of the smaller squares to be sewn in place for the stripes, measure the distance from the corner to the edge of the stripe and add ½" to this measurement.

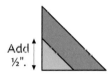

Add ½".

3. Mark a diagonal line on the wrong side of the square for the first stripe and place it right sides together on the corner of the base triangle. Sew on the line and fold over the corner to check for accuracy. Press in the direction indicated by the project instructions and trim away the excess, leaving a ¼" seam allowance.

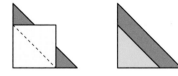

4. Repeat steps 2 and 3 for any remaining stripes.

Side-Striped Triangles

Unlike the other striped pieces we've discussed, side-striped triangles are made by sewing and folding smaller *triangles* to a base unit. Just as with the base of center-striped triangles, you can use half-square or quarter-square triangles; the type you use will depend on where you want the straight grain to fall on the unit.

The process for assembling side-striped triangles isn't much different from making striped squares and rectangles, except that we're working with triangles. Arrows in the diagrams indicate the straight grain of the triangles.

1. For the parent triangle, cut a square once diagonally to make a half-square triangle. To determine the cut size of the square, add ⅞" to the desired finished size of the triangle short edge, just as with any half-square triangle. For this example, we want to create a 3" finished-size striped triangle. Therefore, we cut a 3⅞" parent square and cut it in half diagonally.

2. For the stripes, the straight grain needs to run along the long edge, so you'll need to cut quarter-square triangles. To determine the cut size, measure from the point on the bias edge of the parent triangle to the desired edge of the first stripe. In this case that distance is 2". Double this measurement (2 x 2 = 4) and add 1¼" to determine the cut size of the square needed for the quarter-square triangles (5¼").

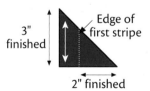

3" finished

Edge of first stripe

2" finished

3. Cut the 5¼" square twice diagonally to make four quarter-square triangles. Mark a center line on one triangle from the center of the long edge to the point where the two short edges meet.

Mark center line on wrong side.

5¼" cut

4. Place the quarter-square triangle on the base of the parent triangle as shown. Stitch on the marked line. Fold the triangle over the corner. Check for accuracy and adjust as necessary. Press and trim away the excess, leaving a ¼" seam allowance.

5. Repeat steps 2–4 for any remaining stripes.

Simple-Striped Triangles

Unlike side-striped triangles, which may look similar, simple-striped triangles are made by folding half-square triangles onto a pieced base unit comprised of two quarter-square triangles. The seam between the quarter-square triangles creates the center strip of the simple-striped triangles.

1. For the parent triangle, cut and sew two quarter-square triangles together to make a pieced triangle base. To determine the cut size of the parent squares for the quarter-square triangles, add 1¼" to the desired finished size of the short edge of the striped triangle. For this example we want to make a 3" finished-size striped triangle. Therefore we cut 4¼"

squares from two different fabrics into quarters diagonally to make the quarter-square triangles to be sewn into pairs.

3" finished triangle

2. For the stripes, the straight grain needs to run along the short edge, so you'll need to cut half-square triangles. To determine the cut size, measure from the narrow point on the pieced triangle to the edge of the stripe. In this case, that is 1½". Add ⅞" to determine the cut size of the half-square triangles (2⅜"). Cut squares in half diagonally to make half-square triangles. Draw a line from the square corner to the center of the long edge.

 1½" Edge of stripe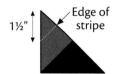

3. Place the half-square triangle on the pieced base triangle as shown. Stitch on the marked line. Fold the triangle over the corner. Check for accuracy and adjust if necessary. Press, and trim away the excess, leaving a ¼" seam allowance.

4. Repeat steps 2–4 for any remaining stripes.

TRY ME QUILTS

Page 26

Page 30

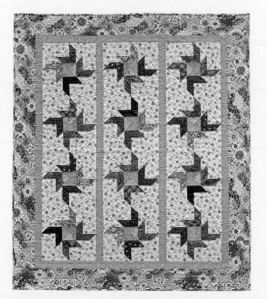

Page 34

Page 39

Taupe Buttons

 These blocks are made in eight sets of 10 using a different pair of dark and medium prints from the same color family for each set. You'll also make six border blocks from each set of prints. It's easy to increase or decrease the size of your quilt by adding or subtracting sets of blocks. If you change the number of blocks you make, you'll need to make more or fewer border blocks for your particular quilt. As long as you don't change the width of the light border between the quilt center and the pieced border, everything will fit. To calculate the number of border blocks you need on each side of your particular quilt, add two to the number of blocks on that side. Total the number of blocks needed for each side and add four for the corners. The result is the total number of border blocks you need.

Finished quilt size: 56½" x 64½"
Finished block size: 4"
Blocks needed: 80 Button and 48 Border

Materials

Yardage is based on 42"-wide fabric.

⅜ yard *each* of 8 dark prints and 8 medium prints for blocks and pieced middle border

1⅜ yards of tan print for inner and outer borders

½ yard of medium taupe fabric for binding

3½ yards of fabric for backing

63" x 71" piece of batting

Cutting

Keep the pieces from each dark and medium print together.

From *each* of the 8 dark prints and 8 medium prints, cut:

1 strip, 5¼" x 42" (16 total); crosscut into 5 squares, 5¼" x 5¼" (80 total). Cut each square into quarters diagonally to make 20 quarter-square triangles (320 total).

1 strip, 1⅞" x 42" (16 total); crosscut into 20 squares, 1⅞" x 1⅞" (320 total)

1 strip, 1½" x 42" (16 total); crosscut into:
6 rectangles, 1½" x 2½" (96 total)
6 rectangles, 1½" x 4½" (96 total)

3 squares, 2½" x 2½" (48 total)

From the tan print, cut:

10 strips, 4½" x 42"

From the medium taupe fabric, cut:

7 strips, 2¼" x 42"

Button Block Assembly

1. Pair the pieces from each dark print with the pieces from a medium print.

2. Working with the pieces from one pair of dark and medium prints, draw a diagonal line on the wrong side of two medium 1⅞" squares. Refer to "Center-Striped Triangles" on page 22 to sew

By Donna Lynn Thomas; machine quilted by Pam Goggans

each square to the corner of a dark quarter-square triangle as shown, right sides together, to make two A center-striped triangles. Press the seam allowances on one center-striped triangle toward the dark print and on the other toward the medium print. Repeat to make a total of 20 A center-striped triangles.

A triangle.
Make 20.

3. Refer to step 2 to sew dark 1⅞" squares to the corners of 20 medium quarter-square triangles to make 20 B center-striped triangles, pressing the seam allowances of 10 triangles in one direction and the remaining 10 triangles in the opposite direction.

B triangle.
Make 20.

4. Lay out two A center-striped triangles and two B center-striped triangles, orienting seam allowances in the directions shown. Sew the triangles into pairs. Press the seam allowances in opposite directions. Sew the pairs together. Press the seam allowances in opposite directions, removing the stitching in the seam allowance at the seam intersection so that all the seam allowances flow counterclockwise. Repeat to make a total of 10 Button blocks. Set aside the remaining pieces for the border blocks.

Button block.
Make 10.

5. Repeat steps 2–4 with each of the remaining pairs of dark and medium prints to make a total of 80 Button blocks.

Border Block Assembly

1. Using the remaining pieces from one pair of dark and medium prints, sew dark 1½" x 2½" rectangles to opposite sides of a medium 2½" square. Press the seam allowances toward the square. Repeat, using the medium rectangles and dark squares. Make three of each.

Make 3.   Make 3.

2. Sew the matching 1½" x 4½" rectangles to the top and bottom of the units from step 1. Press the seam allowances away from the square.

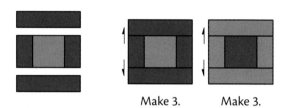

Make 3.   Make 3.

3. Repeat steps 1 and 2 with the remaining pairs of dark and medium prints to make a total of 48 border blocks.

Quilt Top Assembly

1. Referring to the quilt assembly diagram on page 29 and the project photo, lay out the Button blocks in 10 rows of eight blocks each. Experiment with the placement until you achieve a pleasing balance of colors. If you prefer, you can arrange the blocks in diagonal bands of color with dark halves facing each other. Sew the blocks into rows, pressing seam allowances in opposite directions from row to row. Join the rows to complete the center of the quilt.

2. Refer to "Plain Borders" on page 12 to measure and cut the tan 4½"-wide inner-border strips and sew them to the quilt top.

3. Lay out the border blocks in four rows of 12 blocks each, balancing the colors and prints in a pleasing arrangement. Sew the blocks into four border strips. Press the seam allowances in either direction. Sew two strips to the sides of the quilt top. Press the seam allowances toward the tan inner border. Sew the remaining two border strips to the top and bottom edges of the quilt top. Press the seam allowances toward the tan border.

4. Repeat step 2 to add the tan 4½"-wide outer-border strips.

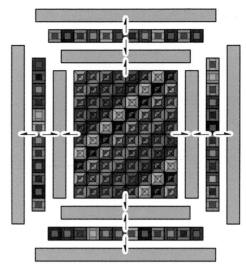

Quilt assembly

Finishing

1. Layer the quilt top with batting and backing; baste the layers together.

2. Quilt as desired.

3. Bind the quilt edges with the medium taupe 2¼"-wide strips.

Color Option

Turtle by David and Gabriel Pursell, 60" x 78"; machine quilted by Sandy Gore. For their quilt, Dave and Gabriel chose a selection of pretty prints that coordinated with a large-scale floral print. Wanting to use the floral fabric for the outer border, they made some changes in the use of plain borders around the pieced center.

Hugs and Kisses

 I designed "Hugs and Kisses" for my son and daughter-in-law, Joe and Katie, as their wedding quilt. Katie loves pink, and the brown is for Joe, but the theme is love! This quilt could just as easily be renamed "Tic-Tac-Toe" and done in pastel pinks for a little girl or blues for a boy. The design goes together easily and is versatile enough that any color theme would work well.

Finished quilt size: 68¾" x 82⅞"
Finished block size: 8"
Blocks needed: 18

Materials

Yardage is based on 42"-wide fabric.

2⅝ yards of brown print for blocks, first and seventh borders, and binding

1¾ yards of white print for blocks and setting triangles

1⅝ yards of red print for blocks and second and sixth borders

1⅛ yards of cream heart print for third and fifth borders

1 yard of pink print for blocks and fourth border

5 yards of fabric for backing

74" x 88" piece of batting

Cutting

From the brown print, cut:

2 strips, 2½" x 42"; crosscut into 18 squares, 2½" x 2½"

6 strips, 3½" x 42"

14 strips, 2¾" x 42"

8 strips, 2¼" x 42"

From the red print, cut:

4 strips, 4" x 42"; crosscut into 36 squares, 4" x 4"

5 strips, 2" x 42"

2 strips, 2½" x 42"; crosscut into 31 squares, 2½" x 2½"

14 strips, 1½" x 42"

From the pink print, cut:

9 strips, 2" x 42"; crosscut *4 of the strips* into 72 squares, 2" x 2"

7 strips, 1½" x 42"

From the white print, cut:

3 strips, 2½" x 42"

4 strips, 4" x 42"; crosscut into 36 squares, 4" x 4"

2 strips, 16" x 42"; crosscut into:

    3 squares, 16" x 16"; cut each square into quarters diagonally to make 12 side setting triangles (you will use 10)

    2 squares, 10" x 10"; cut each square in half diagonally to make 4 corner setting triangles

From the cream heart print, cut:

14 strips, 2½" x 42"

By Donna Lynn Thomas; machine quilted by Kelly Ashton

Strip-Set Assembly

Press seam allowances in the directions indicated by the arrows.

1. Using the five red print and five pink print 2" x 42" strips, assemble five A strip units as shown. Press. Crosscut the strip units into 72 segments, 2½" wide.

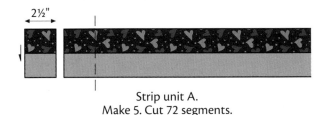

Strip unit A.
Make 5. Cut 72 segments.

2. Using the six brown print 3½" x 42" strips and the three white print 2½" x 42" strips, assemble three B strip units as shown. Press. Crosscut the strip units into 48 segments, 2½" wide.

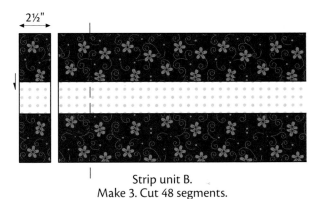

Strip unit B.
Make 3. Cut 48 segments.

Block Assembly

1. Refer to "Add-an-Inch Bias Squares" on page 11 to lay one red and one white 4" square right sides together. Cut the squares in half diagonally to make two pairs of triangles. Sew each triangle pair together along their long edges. Press. Trim each bias square to 3½". Repeat to make a total of 72 bias squares.

Make 72.

2. Refer to "Striped Squares" on page 18 to draw a diagonal line from corner to corner on the wrong side of each pink 2" square. With right sides together, lay a pink square on the red corner of a bias square from step 3. Sew on the diagonal line. Press. Trim away the excess, leaving a ¼" seam allowance. Repeat to make a total of 72 striped squares.

Make 72.

3. Lay out four strip unit A segments, four striped squares, and one brown print 2½" square as shown. Sew the units into rows, and then join the rows to complete the block. Repeat to make a total of 18 blocks.

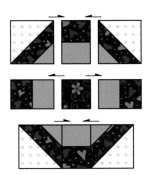 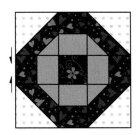

Make 18.

Quilt Top Assembly

1. Arrange the blocks, the strip unit B sashing segments, the red print 2½" squares, and the white print side and corner setting triangles as shown on page 33. Sew the blocks and sashing segments into rows, pressing all of the seam allowances toward the sashing segments. Join the rows to complete the quilt center.

3. Refer to the quilt assembly diagram below and "Plain Borders" on page 12 to measure and cut the brown print 2¾"-wide first-border strips and sew them to the quilt top. In the same manner, measure, cut, and sew the following borders in place in the order listed to complete the top: red 1½"-wide strips, cream 2½"-wide strips, pink 1½"-wide strips, cream 2½"-wide strips, red 1½"-wide strips, and brown 2¾"-wide strips.

Finishing

1. Layer the quilt top with batting and backing; baste the layers together.

2. Quilt as desired.

3. Bind the quilt edges with the brown print 2¼"-wide strips.

2. Trim the sides of the quilt top ¼" from the red print squares.

Quilt assembly

Cupid's Arrows

 The blocks in this quilt are made in three sets of four, with two different pink prints and two different purple prints used in each set of blocks. The four green prints in the block centers appear in all 12 blocks.

Finished quilt size: 49½" x 57¾"
Finished block size: 8"
Blocks needed: 12

Materials

Yardage is based on 42"-wide fabric.
1⅞ yards of light print for blocks and setting triangles
1¼ yards of large-scale floral for outer border and binding
⅛ yard *each* of 6 assorted pink prints for blocks
⅛ yard *each* of 6 assorted purple prints for blocks
⅛ yard *each* of 4 assorted green prints for blocks
½ yard of green print for sashing and inner border
3½ yards of fabric for backing
56" x 64" piece of batting

Cutting

From *each* of the 6 assorted pink prints and 6 assorted purple prints, cut:
1 strip, 2½" x 42" (12 total); crosscut into 8 rectangles, 2½" x 4½" (96 total)

From *each* of the 4 assorted green prints for blocks, cut:
1 strip, 2½" x 42" (4 total); crosscut into 12 squares, 2½" x 2½" (48 total)

From the light print, cut:
9 strips, 2½" x 42"; crosscut into 144 squares, 2½" x 2½"
2 strips, 13" x 42"; crosscut into 5 squares, 13" x 13". Cut each square into quarters diagonally to make 20 side setting triangles (you will use 18).
2 strips, 7" x 42"; crosscut into 6 squares, 7" x 7". Cut each square in half diagonally to make 12 corner setting triangles.

From the green print for sashing, cut:
7 strips, 2" x 42"

From the large-scale floral, cut:
5 strips, 5" x 42"
6 strips, 2¼" x 42"

Block Assembly

Press seam allowances in the directions indicated by the arrows.

1. Draw a diagonal line from corner to corner on the wrong side of each light 2½" square and each green 2½" square.

2. Group the pink and purple rectangles into three sets with each set containing the rectangles from two pink fabrics and two purple fabrics.

3. Working with one set of pink and purple rectangles, refer to "Striped Rectangles" on page 19 to lay a light square from step 1 on the corner of four matching pink rectangles and four matching purple rectangles as shown, right sides together. Sew on the diagonal line. Press. Trim away the excess, leaving a ¼" seam

By Donna Lynn Thomas; machine quilted by Sandy Gore

allowance. Repeat with four rectangles from the remaining pink and purple fabrics.

Make 4 of each pink and purple fabric.

4. Sew another light square to the opposite corner of each unit from step 3 as shown to make four pink and four purple A striped rectangles from each pink and purple fabric. Press.

A striped rectangle.
Make 4 of each pink and purple fabric.

5. Repeat step 3 with the remaining four pink and four purple rectangles of each fabric, but orient the marked line on the light square as shown. Press.

6. Select one set of four matching units from step 5. Refer to step 4 to sew matching green squares to the opposite end of each of these units as shown to make B striped rectangles. Repeat with the remaining units, using a different

green fabric for each set of pink units and each set of purple units.

B striped rectangle.
Make 4 of each pink and purple fabric.

7. Sew matching pink A and B striped rectangles together as shown to make a rectangle square. Orient the A rectangles so their diagonal seams are in the opposite direction of the diagonal seams of the B rectangles. Press. Make four matching rectangle squares. Repeat with the remaining pink and purple A and B striped rectangles.

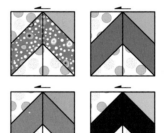

Make 4 matching rectangle squares
of each pink and purple fabric.

8. Lay out one rectangle square of each pink and purple fabric as shown. Sew the squares together to make two rows. Join the rows to make a block. Repeat to make a total of four matching blocks.

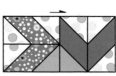

9. Repeat steps 3–8 with the remaining sets to make a total of 12 blocks.

Quilt Top Assembly

1. Arrange the blocks and the light side and corner setting triangles on point into three vertical rows as shown. Balance the position of the different blocks. Sew the blocks and setting triangles together, adding the corner triangles last. Trim the edges of the strips ¼" from the block points.

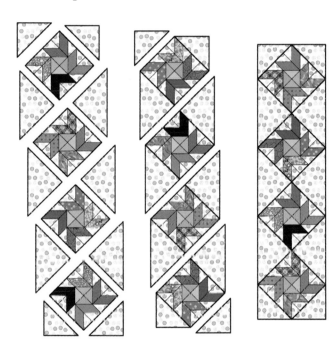

2. Sew the green 2"-wide strips together end to end to make one long strip. Measure the length of the block rows and cut four strips to this measurement from the pieced green strip. Refer to the quilt assembly diagram to alternately sew the block rows and green strips together. Press the seam allowances toward the green strips.

3. Measure the width of the quilt top through the center and cut two strips to this measurement from the remainder of the green pieced strip. Sew the strips to the top and bottom of the quilt. Press the seam allowances toward the green strips.

4. Refer to "Plain Borders" on page 12 to measure and cut the floral 5"-wide outer-border strips and sew them to the quilt top.

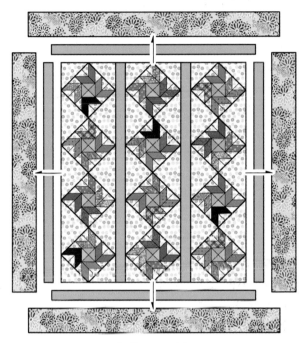

Quilt assembly

Finishing

1. Layer the quilt top with batting and backing; baste the layers together.

2. Quilt as desired.

3. Bind the quilt edges with the floral 2¼"-wide strips.

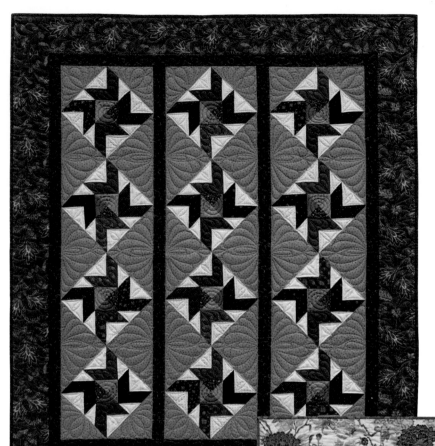

Color Options

Old Time Darts by Kay Harmon, 49½" x 57¾". Using reproduction prints gives this quilt pattern an entirely different look.

Asian Arrows by Donna Lynn Thomas, 53½" x 61¾"; machine quilted by Marilyn Gore. From young and fun to reproduction to Asian, this pattern adapts itself to a myriad of different color and style preferences.

Star Light, Star Bright

These star blocks are made five at a time from different dark and medium prints.

Finished quilt size: 80" x 93½"
Finished block size: 12"
Blocks needed: 20

Materials

Yardage is based on 42"-wide fabric.

2⅛ yards of pale yellow print for block backgrounds

½ yard *each* of 4 assorted medium prints for blocks

1⅞ yards of large-scale blue print for third border

1¾ yards of brown print for sashing squares, second and fourth borders, and binding

⅜ yard *each* of 4 assorted dark prints for blocks

1⅛ yards of tan print for sashing

⅝ yard of striped fabric for first border

⅓ yard of orange print for border corner squares

8 yards of fabric for backing

88" x 102" piece of batting

Cutting

From *each* of the 4 assorted dark prints, cut:

3 strips, 4" x 42" (12 total); crosscut into 30 squares, 4" x 4" (120 total). Cut each square in half diagonally to make 60 half-square triangles (240 total).

From the pale yellow print, cut:

12 strips, 4" x 42"; crosscut into 120 squares, 4" x 4". Cut each square in half diagonally to make 240 half-square triangles.

7 strips, 3" x 42; crosscut into 80 squares, 3" x 3"

From *each* of the 4 assorted medium prints, cut:

1 strip, 6½" x 42" (4 total); crosscut into 5 squares, 6½" x 6½" (20 total)

4 strips, 3" x 42" (16 total); crosscut into 40 squares, 3" x 3" (160 total)

From the tan print, cut:

17 strips, 2" x 42"; crosscut into 49 strips, 2" x 12½"

From the brown print, cut:

18 strips, 2" x 42"; crosscut 2 of the strips into 30 squares, 2" x 2"

9 strips, 2¼" x 42"

From the striped fabric, cut:

7 strips, 2½" x 42"

From the large-scale blue print, cut:

8 strips, 7½" x 42"

From the orange print, cut:

1 strip, 7½" x 42"; crosscut into:

  4 squares, 7½" x 7½"

  4 squares, 2½" x 2½"

  8 squares, 2" x 2"

Block Assembly

Press seam allowances in the directions indicated by the arrows.

1. Using the triangles from one dark print and referring to "Add-an-Inch Bias Squares" on page 11, sew each dark triangle to a pale yellow triangle along the long edges to make 60 bias squares. Press 30 seam allowances toward the dark print and 30 toward the yellow print. Trim the bias squares to 3½". Sort the trimmed bias squares by pressing direction.

Make 30. Make 30.

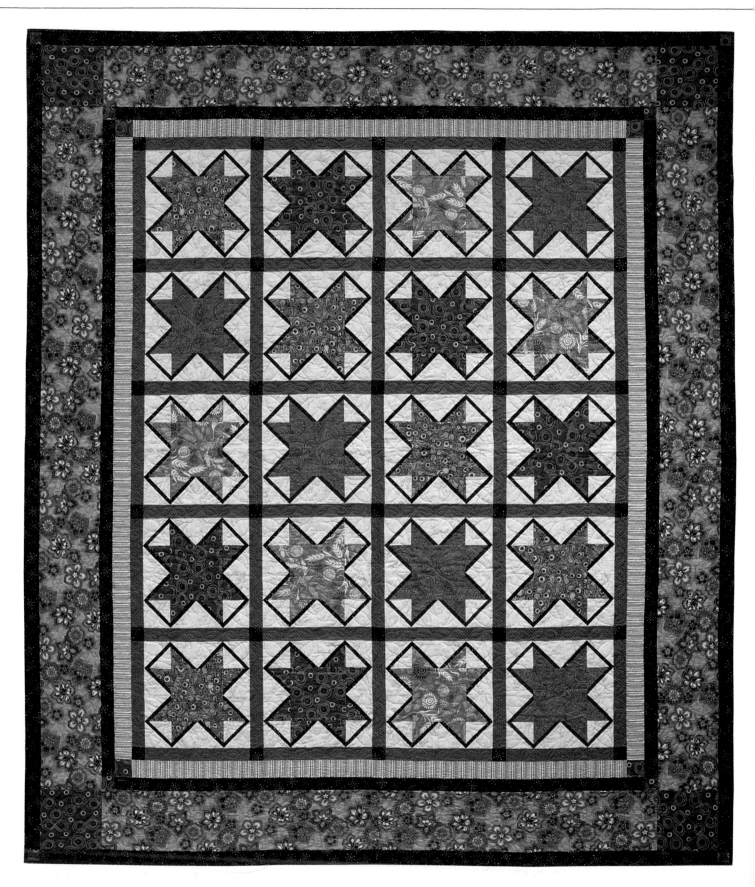

By Donna Lynn Thomas; machine quilted by Kim Pope

2. Select 10 bias squares from step 1 that are pressed toward the yellow print and 10 that are pressed toward the dark print. Draw a diagonal line from corner to corner on the wrong side of 20 pale yellow squares. With right sides together, lay a marked yellow square on the dark corner of a bias square as shown. Stitch on the line. Trim away the excess, leaving a ¼" seam allowance. Press the seam allowances in the direction of the original bias square seam. Repeat to make a total of 20 units.

Make 10.   Make 10.

3. On each 3" square cut from one medium print, draw a diagonal line on the wrong side. With right sides together, lay a marked square on the dark corner of one of the remaining bias squares from step 1 as shown. Stitch on the line. Trim away the excess, leaving a ¼" seam allowance. Press the seam allowances in the same direction as the bias square seam. Repeat with the remaining bias squares to make a total of 20 units with the seam allowances pressed toward the yellow and 20 units with the seam allowances pressed toward the dark.

Make 10.   Make 10.

4. Paying careful attention to the pressing direction of each of the units from steps 2 and 3, lay out four units from step 2, eight units from step 3, and one medium print 6½" square as shown. Sew the pieces into rows. Press. Join the rows to make a block. Press. Repeat to

make a total of five matching Star Light, Star Bright blocks.

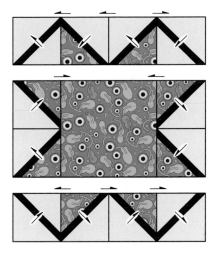

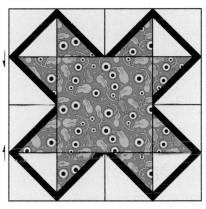

Make 5.

5. Repeat steps 1–4 to make a total of 20 Star Light, Star Bright blocks.

Quilt Top Assembly

1. Refer to the quilt assembly diagram on page 42 to lay out the blocks, the tan 2" x 12½" sashing strips, and the brown print 2" sashing squares into block rows and sashing rows. Arrange the blocks to form diagonal lines of color across the quilt. Sew the pieces in each row together, and press the seam allowances toward the sashing strips. Join the rows to complete the center of the quilt. Press the seam allowances toward the sashing rows.

2. Sew the striped strips together end to end to make one long strip. Measure the length of the quilt top through the quilt center. From the pieced strip, cut two strips to this measurement for the side borders. Measure the width of the quilt top through the quilt center and cut two strips to this measurement for the top and bottom borders. Sew the side borders to the sides of the quilt top. Press the seam allowances toward the border strips. Add an orange print 2½" square to each end of the top and bottom border strips. Press the seam allowances toward the squares. Sew the strips to the top and bottom of the quilt top. Press the seam allowances toward the border strips.

3. Repeat step 2 with the brown print 2"-wide strips for the second border, the blue print strips for the third border, and the remaining brown print 2"-wide strips for the fourth border, using corner squares that correspond to the width of each strip.

Finishing

1. Layer the quilt top with batting and backing; baste the layers together.

2. Quilt as desired.

3. Bind the quilt edges with the brown print 2¼"-wide strips.

Quilt assembly

Color Option

Happy Stars by Beth Woods, 80" x 93½"; machine quilted by Denise Mariano. Beth used a collection of soft, pretty prints in blue and brown to make her lovely quilt.

GROW WITH ME QUILTS

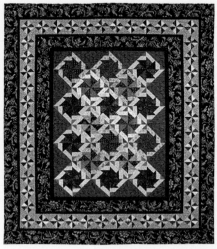

Page 44

Page 49

Page 54

Page 59

Page 64

Warm Winds

 Reminiscent of warmly nostalgic days gone by, these traditional Windmill blocks are complemented nicely by the pinwheel border, which is made completely from leftover block pieces. The blocks in this quilt are made in pairs using two color combinations.

Finished quilt size: 80½" x 91⅝"
Finished Windmill Block: 10"
Finished Pinwheel Block: 4"
Blocks needed: 18 Windmill and 48 Pinwheel

Materials

Yardage is based on 42"-wide fabric.
⅓ yard *each* of 9 assorted cream prints, 6 assorted blue prints, and 3 assorted brown prints for blocks
3¼ yards of large-scale blue print for second border, sixth border, and binding
¼ yard *each* of 6 assorted red prints and 3 assorted pink prints for blocks
1¼ yards of tan print for pieced fourth border
1⅛ yards of red print for first, third, and fifth borders
1 yard of brown print for setting triangles
9" square *each* of 9 assorted green prints for blocks
8 yards of fabric for backing
86" x 98" piece of batting

Cutting

From *each* of the 9 assorted cream prints, cut:
2 squares, 6¼" x 6¼" (18 total); cut each square into quarters diagonally to make 8 quarter-square triangles (72 total)
4 squares, 5⅞" x 5⅞" (36 total); cut each square in half diagonally to make 8 half-square triangles (72 total)
7 squares, 3" x 3" (63 total); cut each square in half diagonally to make 14 half-square triangles (126 total; you will use 120)

From *each* of the 6 assorted red prints and 3 assorted pink prints, cut:
2 squares, 6¼" x 6¼" (18 total); cut each square into quarters diagonally to make 8 quarter-square triangles (72 total)

From *each* of the 9 assorted green prints, cut:
4 squares, 3⅝" x 3⅝" (36 total); cut each square in half diagonally to make 8 half-square triangles (72 total)

From *each* of the 6 assorted blue prints, cut:
2 squares, 8¼" x 8¼" (12 total); cut each square into quarters diagonally to make 8 quarter-square triangles (48 total)
5 squares, 3" x 3" (30 total); cut each square in half diagonally to make 10 half-square triangles (60 total)

From *each* of the 3 assorted brown prints, cut:
2 squares, 8¼" x 8¼" (6 total); cut each square into quarters diagonally to make 8 quarter-square triangles (24 total)
10 squares, 3" x 3" (30 total); cut each square in half diagonally to make 20 half-square triangles (60 total)

By Donna Lynn Thomas; machine quilted by Freda Smith

From the brown print for setting triangles, cut:

3 squares, 16" x 16"; cut each square into quarters diagonally to make 12 side setting triangles (you will use 10)

2 squares, 8½" x 8½"; cut each square in half diagonally to make 4 corner setting triangles

From the red print for borders, cut:

6 strips, 2" x 42"

15 strips, 1½" x 42"

From the large-scale blue print, cut:

4 strips, 5⅛" x 42"

3 strips, 3⅝" x 42"

9 strips, 5½" x 42"

9 strips, 2¼" x 42"

From the tan print, cut:

1 strip, 3⅞" x 42"; crosscut into 8 squares, 3⅞" x 3⅞". Cut each square in half diagonally to make 16 half-square triangles.

5 strips, 7" x 42"; crosscut into 22 squares, 7" x 7". Cut each square into quarters diagonally to make 88 quarter-square triangles.

Block Assembly

Press seam allowances in the directions indicated by the arrows.

1. Select eight matching cream quarter-square triangles and half-square triangles, eight matching red quarter-square triangles, eight matching green half-square triangles, and eight matching blue quarter-square triangles.

2. Working with the pieces from step 1, sew a cream quarter-square triangle to a red quarter-square triangle as shown. Repeat to make a total of eight units.

Make 8.

3. Refer to "Simple-Striped Triangles" on page 24 to draw a line on the wrong side of each green half-square triangle as shown.

4. With right sides together, lay a marked green triangle on the cream side of a unit from step 2 as shown. Sew on the line. Press. Trim away the excess, leaving a ¼" seam allowance. Repeat with the remaining units from step 2 to make eight simple-striped triangles.

Make 8.

5. Repeat step 3 with the blue quarter-square triangles.

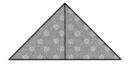

6. With right sides together, lay a marked blue triangle on a cream half-square triangle as shown. Sew on the line. Press. Trim away the excess, leaving a ¼" seam allowance. Reserve the trim-away triangle pair for use later in the pieced border. Repeat to make a total of eight units.

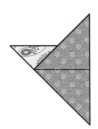

7. Sew a unit from step 4 to a unit from step 6 as shown to make a quarter block. Repeat to make a total of eight quarter blocks.

8. Sew four quarter blocks together as shown to complete one Windmill block. Repeat to make a total of two blocks.

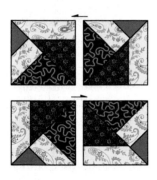 

Make 12.

9. Repeat steps 2–8 to make a total of 12 blocks.

10. Repeat steps 1–8, substituting a pink print for the red print and a brown print for the blue print to make six additional blocks.

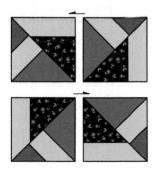 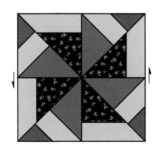

Make 6.

Quilt Top Assembly

1. Lay out the blocks, 10 brown side setting triangles, and four brown corner setting triangles into diagonal rows, positioning the brown-and-pink blocks in the center as shown. Sew the blocks and setting pieces into rows, pressing the seam allowances in alternate directions from row to row. Join the rows to form the quilt center.

2. Trim the quilt top ¼" from the block points.

3. Refer to "Plain Borders" on page 12 to measure and cut red 2"-wide first-border strips and sew them to the quilt top. Repeat to add the blue print 5⅛"-wide second-border strips to the sides of the quilt top and the blue print 3⅝"-wide second-border strips to the top and bottom of the quilt top. These strips are different widths to accommodate the pieced border. Add the red 1½"-wide third-border strips to the quilt top in the same manner.

4. Refer to "Add-an-Inch Bias Squares" on page 11 to sew the 72 brown-and-cream and

blue-and-cream reserved trim-away triangle pairs together along their long edges. Press. Randomly sew a cream 3" half-square triangle to each brown and each blue 3" half-square triangle to make 120 more bias squares. You will have six leftover cream triangles. Including the trim-away bias squares, you should have a total of 192 bias squares. Trim each bias square to 2½".

5. Sew two blue and two brown bias squares together as shown to make a Pinwheel block. Press. Repeat to make a total of 48 Pinwheel blocks.

Make 48.

6. Lay out 12 Pinwheel blocks, 22 tan quarter-square triangles, and four tan half-square triangles as shown. Sew the triangles to the blocks, and then sew the block units together. Repeat to make four pieced borders. Trim the border strips ¼" from the block points.

Make 4.

7. Refer to the quilt assembly diagram below and "Pieced Borders" on page 13 to sew two pieced border strips from step 6 to the sides of the quilt top. Press the seam allowances toward the red border. Sew the two remaining pieced border strips to the top and bottom of the quilt top. Press the seam allowances toward the red border.

8. Refer to "Plain Borders" to measure and cut the remaining red 1½"-wide fifth-border strips and sew them to the quilt top, followed by the blue print 5½"-wide sixth-border strips. Press.

Quilt assembly

Finishing

1. Layer the quilt top with batting and backing; baste the layers together.

2. Quilt as desired.

3. Bind the quilt edges with the blue print 2¼"-wide strips.

Flames

 The key to choosing fabrics for this block is to grade the four prints in each striped rectangle from dark to light using one color family. Although I used vibrant orange, this quilt would be lovely in any number of fabric themes such as pastels, batiks, or reproduction prints.

Finished quilt size: 65½" x 65½"
Finished block size: 12"
Blocks needed: 13

Materials

Yardage is based on 42"-wide fabric.
2½ yards of black print for blocks, setting triangles, and fourth border
1⅓ yards of red print for blocks, third border, and binding
1⅛ yards of dark orange print for blocks and second border
1⅛ yards of medium orange print for blocks and first border
⅞ yard of light gray print for blocks and pieced side setting triangles
⅔ yard of medium gray print for blocks and pieced side setting triangles
⅔ yard of pale yellow print for blocks
⅝ yard of light orange print for blocks
4½ yards of fabric for backing
72" x 72" square of batting

Cutting

From the red print, cut:
7 strips, 2½" x 42"; crosscut into 104 squares, 2½" x 2½"
6 strips, 1½" x 42"
7 strips, 2¼" x 42"

From the dark orange print, cut:
10 strips, 2½" x 42"; crosscut into 104 rectangles, 2½" x 3½"
6 strips, 1½" x 42"

From the medium orange print, cut:
10 strips, 2½" x 42"; crosscut into 104 rectangles, 2½" x 3½"
6 strips, 1½" x 42"

From the light orange print, cut:
7 strips, 2½" x 42"; crosscut into 104 squares, 2½" x 2½"

From the pale yellow print, cut:
4 strips, 5" x 42"; crosscut into 26 squares, 5" x 5". Cut each square in half diagonally to make 52 half-square triangles.

From the light gray print, cut:
4 strips, 5" x 42"; crosscut into 26 squares, 5" x 5". Cut each square in half diagonally to make 52 half-square triangles.
1 strip, 4½" x 42"; crosscut into 8 squares, 4½" x 4½"

From the black print, cut:

2 strips, 4½" x 42"; crosscut into 13 squares,
  4½" x 4½"

4 strips, 2½" x 42"; crosscut into 60 squares,
  2½" x 2½"

2 squares, 19½" x 19½"; cut each square into
  quarters diagonally to make 8 side setting
  triangles

2 squares, 10" x 10"; cut each square in half
  diagonally to make 4 corner setting triangles

7 strips, 4½" x 42"

From the medium gray print, cut:

6 strips, 3½" x 42"; crosscut into 60 squares,
  3½" x 3½"

Block Assembly

Press all seam allowances in the direction of the
arrows.

1. Refer to "Striped Rectangles" on page 19 to
   draw a diagonal line from corner to corner
   on the wrong side of each red square. With
   right sides together, lay a marked square on a
   dark orange rectangle as shown. Sew on the
   line. Trim away the excess, leaving a ¼" seam
   allowance. Repeat to make a total of 104 units.
   Press 52 of the seam allowances toward the
   dark print and 52 toward the medium print.

Make 52.   Make 52.

2. Draw a 45° diagonal line on the wrong side
   of each medium orange rectangle. With right
   sides together, lay a marked rectangle on a unit
   from step 1 as shown. Sew on the line. Trim
   away the excess, leaving a ¼" seam allowance.
   Press in the same direction as the previous

seam allowances. Repeat with the remaining
units from step 1.

Make 52.   Make 52.

3. Draw a diagonal line on the wrong side of
   each light orange 2½" square. With right
   sides together, lay a marked square on a unit
   from step 2 as shown. Sew on the line. Trim
   away the excess, leaving a ¼" seam allowance.
   Press in the same direction as the previous
   seam allowances. Repeat with the remaining
   units from step 2. Sort the completed striped
   rectangles by pressing direction.

Make 52.   Make 52.

4. Arrange four rectangles pressed toward the
   light corner and four rectangles pressed toward
   the dark corner into pairs, carefully orienting
   the pressing directions as shown to make
   units A and B. Sew the rectangles in each pair
   together. Press. Repeat to make a total of 26 A
   units and 26 B units.

A unit.   B unit.
Make 26.   Make 26.

5. Refer to "Add-an-Inch Bias Squares" on page 11
   to sew a pale yellow 5" triangle to a light gray
   5" triangle along their long edges. Repeat to
   make a total of 52 bias squares. Press 26 seam

By Donna Lynn Thomas; machine quilted by Darlene Szabo

allowances toward the gray print and 26 toward the yellow print. Trim each bias square to 4½".

Make 26.   Make 26.

6. Refer to "Striped Squares" on page 18 to draw a diagonal line from corner to corner on the wrong side of each medium gray square. With right sides together, lay a marked square on the light gray side of a bias square from step 5 as shown. Sew on the line. Trim away the excess, leaving a ¼" seam allowance. Repeat with the remaining bias squares. Press the seam allowances in the direction of the previous seam allowances. Set aside the remaining eight medium gray marked squares.

Make 26.   Make 26.

7. Draw a diagonal line from corner to corner on the wrong side of each black 2½" square. With right sides together, lay a marked square on the medium gray side of a striped square from step 6 as shown. Sew on the line. Trim away the excess, leaving a ¼" seam allowance. Repeat with the remaining striped squares. Press the seam allowances in the direction of the previous seam allowances. Sort the completed striped squares by pressing direction. Set aside the remaining eight black marked squares.

Make 26.   Make 26.

8. Lay out two A units, two B units, two striped squares pressed toward the dark print, two striped squares pressed toward the yellow print, and one black 4½" square as shown. Sew the patches into rows. Join the rows to complete a block. Press. Repeat to make a total of 13 blocks.

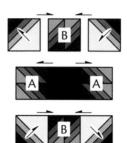 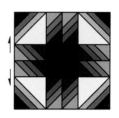

Make 13.

Side Setting Triangle Assembly

1. Refer to "Center-Striped Triangles" on page 22 to draw a diagonal line from corner to corner on the wrong side of each light gray 4½" square. With right sides together, lay a marked square on a black side setting triangle as shown. Sew on the line. Trim away the excess, leaving a ¼" seam allowance. Press. Repeat to make a total of eight units.

2. In the same fashion, mark, sew, trim, and press a medium gray 3½" square to the unit from step 1, followed by a black 2½" square as shown.

Make 8.

Quilt Top Assembly

1. Lay out the blocks, the striped side setting triangles, and the black corner setting triangles in diagonal rows as shown. Sew the blocks into rows, pressing the seam allowances in alternate directions from row to row. Join the rows to form the quilt center. Trim the edges of the quilt ¼" from the block corners.

Quilt assembly

2. Refer to "Plain Borders" on page 12 and the quilt assembly diagram above right to measure and cut the medium orange 1½"-wide first-border strips and sew them to the quilt top. Repeat with the dark orange 1½"-wide second-border strips, the red 1½"-wide third-border strips, and then the black 4½"-wide fourth-border strips.

Finishing

1. Layer the quilt top with batting and backing; baste the layers together.

2. Quilt as desired.

3. Bind the quilt edges with the red 2¼"-wide strips.

Color Option

Brianne's Sunflowers by Kim Pope, 66½" x 66½". The lovely brown, gold, and green colors of Kim's quilt truly reflect the lovely sunflowers that cover the Kansas countryside in late summer. Kim adjusted her border sizes to fit the dimensions of her particular quilt. This will be a wedding gift to Kim's daughter.

Shimmering Leaves

 This pattern is easily adaptable to make a quilt that fits your needs. The blocks are constructed one at a time from sets of dark, medium, and light leaf-colored prints. The same background fabric is used for all the blocks, although you could choose to vary those as well.

Finished quilt size: 58½" x 74½"
Finished block size: 8"
Blocks needed: 24

Materials

Yardage is based on 42"-wide fabric.
24 sets of 10" x 10" squares for blocks and pieced fifth border, each set consisting of 1 light, 1 medium, and 1 dark leaf-colored print from the same color family
1⅛ yards of light print for block backgrounds
1⅛ yards of tan print 2 for third border
1⅛ yards of brown print for second border, fourth border, and binding
½ yard of tan print 1 for first border
4 yards of fabric for backing
64" x 80" piece of batting

Cutting

For ease in piecing, work with one set of leaf-colored pieces at a time and keep them in their original sets after cutting.

From *each* of the 24 dark leaf-colored squares, cut:
6 squares, 2½" x 2½" (144 total)
1 rectangle, 2½" x 4½" (24 total)

From *each* of the 24 medium leaf-colored squares, cut:
4 rectangles, 2½" x 3½" (96 total)
1 square, 2" x 2" (24 total)

From *each* of the 24 light leaf-colored squares, cut:
4 rectangles, 2½" x 3½" (96 total)
1 rectangle, 1" x 2½" (24 total)
1 rectangle, 1" x 2" (24 total)

From the remainder of the dark and medium leaf-colored prints, cut a *total* of:
116 rectangles, 2½" x 4½"
4 squares, 4½" x 4½"

From the light background print, cut:
11 strips, 2½" x 42"; crosscut into:
    120 squares, 2½" x 2½"
    24 rectangles, 2½" x 4½"
3 strips, 2¼" x 42"; crosscut into 48 squares, 2¼" x 2¼"

From tan print 1, cut:
5 strips, 2½" x 42"

From the brown print, cut:
12 strips, 1½" x 42"
7 strips, 2¼" x 42"

From tan print 2, cut:
6 strips, 5½" x 42"

Block Assembly

Press all seam allowances in the direction of the arrows.

1. Referring to "Striped Rectangles" on page 19 and working with the pieces from one set of light, medium, and dark leaf-colored prints, draw a diagonal line from corner to corner on the wrong side of a dark 2½" square. With right sides together, lay the marked square on a

By Donna Lynn Thomas; machine quilted by Pam Goggans

medium 2½" x 3½" rectangle as shown. Sew on the line. Press. Trim away the excess, leaving a ¼" seam allowance. Repeat to make a total of two units.

Make 2.

2. Draw a 45° diagonal line on the wrong side of a light 2½" x 3½" rectangle. With right sides together, lay a marked rectangle on a unit from step 1 as shown. Sew on the line. Trim away the excess, leaving a ¼" seam allowance. Repeat with the remaining unit from step 1.

Make 2.

3. Draw a diagonal line from corner to corner on the wrong side of a background 2½" square. With right sides together, lay it on a unit from step 2 as shown. Sew on the line. Press. Trim away the excess, leaving a ¼" seam allowance. Repeat with the remaining unit from step 2.

Make 2.

4. Repeat steps 1–3, orienting the lines on the marked squares and rectangles as shown to create two mirror-image units.

Make 2.

5. Draw a diagonal line on the wrong side of two background 2¼" squares. With right sides together, place a marked square on a dark 2½" square as shown. Sew on the line. Press. Trim away the excess, leaving a ¼" seam allowance. In the same fashion, sew the second marked square to the opposite corner of the unit as shown to make a stem unit.

6. Sew the light 1" x 2" rectangle to the side of the medium 2" square as shown. Press. Sew the light 1" x 2½" rectangle to the top of the unit. Press.

7. Lay out the units from steps 3, 4, 5, and 6, the remaining dark rectangle and square from the set, and a background 2½" x 4½" rectangle and 2½" square as shown. Sew the units in each quadrant together. Press. Join the quadrants into rows. Press. Join the rows to make a Shimmering Leaves block. Remove the stitching in the seam allowance at the center point so that all the seam allowances flow counterclockwise.

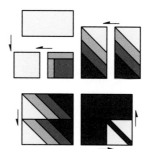 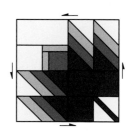

8. Repeat steps 1–7 with the remaining sets of leaf-colored squares to make a total of 24 blocks.

Quilt Top Assembly

1. Lay out the blocks in six rows of four blocks each. Sew the blocks into rows. Press the seam allowances in alternate directions from row to row. Join the rows to form the quilt center.

2. Refer to "Plain Borders" on page 12 and the quilt assembly diagram at right to measure, cut, and sew the borders to the quilt in the following order. Press the seam allowances toward the newly added border strips after each addition: 2½"-wide tan 1 first-border strips, 1½"-wide brown second-border strips, 5½"-wide tan 2 third-border strips, and 1½"-wide brown fourth-border strips.

3. Refer to "Pieced Borders" on page 13 and the quilt assembly diagram to assemble and sew 33 dark and medium rectangles together along their long edges. Repeat to make a total of two border strips. Sew the strips to the sides of the quilt top. Press the seam allowances toward the brown fourth border. Sew 25 dark and medium rectangles together in the same manner for the top border. Repeat to make the bottom border. Add a dark or medium 4½" square to each end of the border strips. Sew the strips to the top and bottom of the quilt top. Press the seam allowances toward the brown fourth border.

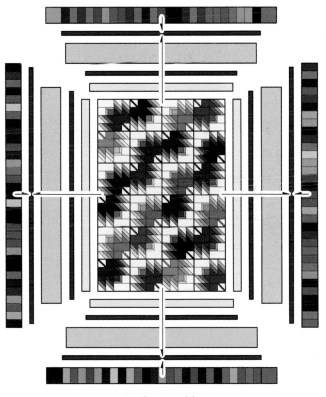

Quilt assembly

Finishing

1. Layer the quilt top with batting and backing; baste the layers together.

2. Quilt as desired.

3. Bind the quilt edges with the brown 2¼"-wide strips.

Color Option

Come September **by Ysleta Meeks, 58½" x 74½"; machine quilted by Nan Doljac. Ysleta's quilt welcomes autumn with vibrant color that just radiate joy. A plain multicolored border offsets the center perfectly.**

More Color Options

Winter Fall by Donna Lynn Thomas, 32½" x 32½"; hand quilted by Shirley Jenkins. A four-block version of the featured quilt is just the right size for displaying on a wall or table.

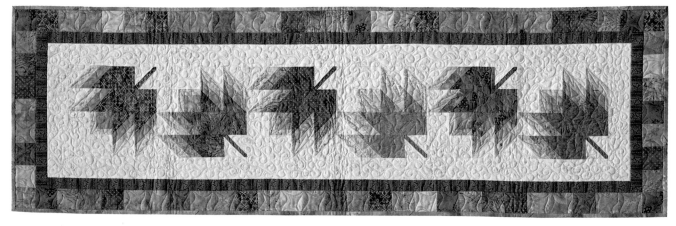

Spring Leaves by Donna Lynn Thomas, 18½" x 58½"; machine quilted by Kim Pope. This monochromatic color scheme is perfect for capturing the essence of spring. Vary the number of blocks to fit your needs.

Blades

 This block is not difficult to make, and when set together without sashings a secondary design pops up. The beautiful border print was the inspiration for the colors I used. My son, an Army Kiowa aviator, contributed to naming this quilt because it reminded him of his helicopter rotors . . . which I mistakenly call blades.

Finished quilt size: 73" x 87"
Finished block size: 10"
Blocks needed: 18

Materials

Yardage is based on 42"-wide fabric.
2⅞ yards of white print for block piecing
2⅜ yards of black batik for first, third, and fifth borders and binding
1⅞ yards of large-scale multicolored print for fourth border
1⅝ yards of black dot print for blocks
1⅛ yards of blue print for blocks
1 yard of purple print for blocks and second border
⅝ yard of green print for blocks
5½ yards of fabric for backing
79" x 93" piece of batting

Cutting

From the blue print, cut:
12 strips, 3" x 42"; crosscut into 144 squares, 3" x 3"

From the white print, cut:
12 strips, 4¼" x 42"; crosscut into 144 rectangles, 3" x 4¼"
6 strips, 3" x 42"; crosscut into 72 squares, 3" x 3"
3 strips, 8⅜" x 42"; crosscut into 12 squares, 8⅜" x 8⅜". Cut each square in half diagonally to make 24 half-square triangles.

From the black dot print, cut:
12 strips, 4¼" x 42"; crosscut into 144 rectangles, 3" x 4¼"

From the green print, cut:
6 strips, 3" x 42"; crosscut into 72 squares, 3" x 3"

From the purple print, cut:
4 strips, 2" x 42"; crosscut into 72 squares, 2" x 2"
6 strips, 3½" x 42"

From the black batik, cut:
6 strips, 2½" x 42"
15 strips, 2" x 42"
3 strips, 4¼" x 42"; crosscut into 24 squares, 4¼" x 4¼"
9 strips, 2¼" x 42"

From the large-scale multicolored print, cut:
8 strips, 7½" x 42"

Block Assembly

Press all seam allowances in the direction of the arrows.

1. Refer to "Striped Rectangles" on page 19 to draw a diagonal line from corner to corner on the wrong side of each blue 3" square. With

right sides together, lay a marked square on a white rectangle as shown. Sew on the line. Press. Trim away the excess, leaving a ¼" seam allowance. Repeat to make a total of 72 units. Set aside the remaining marked squares.

Make 72.

2. Draw a 45° diagonal line on the wrong side of each black dot rectangle as shown. With right sides together, lay a marked rectangle on a unit from step 1 as shown. Sew on the line. Press. Trim away the excess, leaving a ¼" seam allowance. Repeat with the remaining units from step 1. Set aside the remaining marked rectangles.

Make 72.

3. Draw a diagonal line from corner to corner on the wrong side of each green 3" square. With right sides together, lay a marked square on a unit from step 2 as shown. Sew on the line. Press. Trim away the excess, leaving a ¼" seam allowance. Repeat with the remaining units from step 2.

Make 72.

4. Draw a diagonal line from corner to corner on the wrong side of each purple 2" square. With right sides together, lay a marked square on a unit from step 3 as shown. Sew on the line. Press. Trim away the excess, leaving a ¼" seam allowance. Repeat with the remaining units from step 3 to make 72 A rectangles.

A rectangle.
Make 72.

5. With right sides together, lay a marked blue square that you set aside in step 1 on a white rectangle as shown. Sew on the line. Press. Trim away the excess, leaving a ¼" seam allowance. Repeat to make a total of 72 units.

Make 72.

6. With right sides together, lay a marked black dot rectangle that you set aside in step 2 on a unit from step 5 as shown. Sew on the line. Press. Trim away the excess, leaving a ¼" seam allowance. Repeat with the remaining units from step 5.

Make 72.

By Donna Lynn Thomas; machine quilted by Sandy Gore

7. Draw a diagonal line from corner to corner on the wrong side of each white 3" square. With right sides together, lay a marked square on a unit from step 6 as shown. Sew on the line. Press. Trim away the excess, leaving a ¼" seam allowance. Repeat with the remaining units from step 6 to make a total of 72 B rectangles.

B rectangle.
Make 72.

8. Sew each A rectangle to a B rectangle, sewing from the edge where the diagonal seams meet. Make sure the diagonal seam allowances oppose to make perfect intersections. Make 72 rectangle pairs.

Make 72.

9. Lay out four rectangle pairs as shown. Sew the pairs into rows. Press. Sew the rows together to make a Blades block. Remove the stitching in the seam allowance at the center point and press the seam allowances in a clockwise direction. Repeat to make a total of 18 blocks.

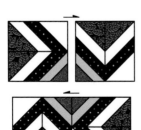 

Make 18.

Setting Triangle Assembly

1. Refer to "Center-Striped Triangles" on page 22 to draw a diagonal line on the wrong side of each black batik 4¼" square. With right sides together, lay a marked black square on the corner of a white 8⅜" triangle as shown. Sew on the line. Press. Trim away the excess, leaving a ¼" seam allowance. Repeat to make a total of 24 center-striped triangles. Press the seam allowances on 10 triangles toward the white and on 14 toward the black.

Make 10.   Make 14.

2. Sew 20 of the center-striped triangles into pairs as shown, using one triangle pressed in each direction to make each pair. Orient the triangles as shown according to their pressing directions. Reserve the remaining four center-striped triangles for the corner setting triangles.

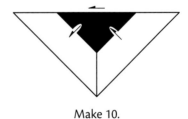

Make 10.

Quilt Top Assembly

1. Lay out the blocks and the side and corner striped setting triangles into diagonal rows as shown. Sew the blocks into rows. Press the seam allowances in alternate directions from row to row. Join the rows to form the quilt center. Trim the quilt top ¼" from the block points.

2. Refer to "Plain Borders" on page 12 to measure and cut the black 2½"-wide first-border strips and sew them to the quilt top. Press the seam allowances toward the border. In the same fashion, add the purple 3½"-wide second-border strips, the black batik 2"-wide third-border strips, the multicolored print 7½"-wide fourth-border strips, and the black batik 2"-wide fifth-border strips to the quilt top.

Quilt assembly

Finishing

1. Layer the quilt top with batting and backing; baste the layers together.

2. Quilt as desired.

3. Bind the quilt edges with the black batik 2¼"-wide strips.

Fractured Glass

 This block is so much fun to make. The possibilities for color are endless. Make the blocks in pairs from eight different sets of black and bright prints. The black serves to frame the colors like stained glass and the fact that the block lines don't meet provides a disjointed, fractured look. The sawtooth border is composed of leftovers from making the blocks.

Finished quilt size: 65½" x 65½"
Finished block size: 9"
Blocks needed: 16

Materials

Yardage is based on 42"-wide fabric.

2⅛ yards of black print for first, third, fifth, and seventh borders and binding

1½ yards of light green print for blocks and second border

⅝ yard *each* of 8 assorted black prints for blocks and fourth and sixth pieced borders

⅜ yard *each* of 8 assorted bright prints for blocks and fourth and sixth pieced borders

4½ yards of fabric for backing

72" x 72" square of batting

Cutting

From *each* of the 8 assorted bright prints, cut:

1 strip, 9⅛" x 42" (8 total); crosscut into 4 squares, 9⅛" x 9⅛" (32 total). Cut each square in half diagonally to make 8 half-square triangles (64 total).

From *each* of the 8 assorted black prints, cut:

2 squares, 10¼" x 10¼" (16 total); cut each square into quarters diagonally to make 8 quarter-square triangles (64 total)

4 squares, 6⅞" x 6⅞" (32 total); cut each square in half diagonally to make 8 half-square triangles (64 total)

4 squares, 3⅞" x 3⅞" (32 total); cut each square in half diagonally to make 8 half-square triangles (64 total)

From the light green print, cut:

6 strips, 6⅛" x 42"; crosscut into 32 squares, 6⅛" x 6⅛". Cut each square in half diagonally to make 64 half-square triangles.

5 strips, 2" x 42"

From the black print for borders and binding, cut:

9 strips, 1¾" x 42"

6 strips, 2" x 42"

7 strips, 3½" x 42"

7 strips, 2¼" x 42"

Block Assembly

Press all seam allowances in the direction of the arrows. Pay careful attention to triangle orientation in the diagrams, as it's easy to become confused.

1. Group the assorted bright and assorted black triangles into sets, with each set consisting of the triangles from one bright print and one black print.

By Donna Lynn Thomas; machine quilted by Freda Smith

2. Working with one set of pieces, refer to "Side-Striped Triangles" on page 23 to draw a line on the wrong side of each bright print half-square triangle as shown. With right sides together, lay a marked triangle on a black 10¼" quarter-square triangle as shown. Stitch on the line. Press. Trim away the excess, leaving a ¼" seam allowance. Set aside the trim-away triangle pairs. Repeat to make a total of eight units.

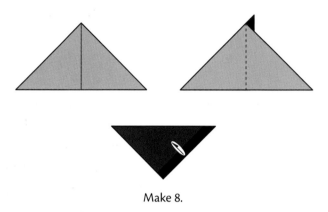

Make 8.

3. Cut the trim-away triangle pairs you set aside in step 2 in half from the square corner to the center of the long edge as shown to create two pairs of triangles. Referring to "Add-an-Inch Bias Squares" on page 11, sew each pair together along their long edges to make a total of 16 bias squares. Press. Trim the bias squares to 3½" and set them aside for the pieced borders.

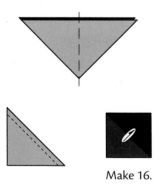

Make 16.

4. Draw a line on the wrong side of each black 6⅞" half-square triangle as shown. With right sides together, lay a marked triangle on a unit from step 2 as shown. Stitch on the line. Press. Trim away the excess, leaving a ¼" seam allowance. Repeat with the remaining units from step 2. Set aside two trim-away triangle pairs.

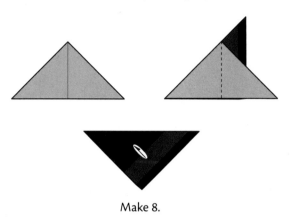

Make 8.

5. Refer to "Add-an-Inch Bias Squares" to sew the two pairs of trim-away triangles together along their long edges to make two bias squares. Trim each bias square to 3½" and set them aside for the pieced borders.

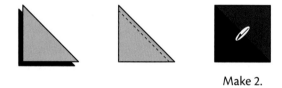

Make 2.

6. Draw a line on the wrong side of eight light green 6⅛" half-square triangles as shown. With right sides together, lay a marked triangle on a unit from step 4 as shown. Stitch on the line. Press. Trim away the excess, leaving a ¼" seam allowance. Repeat with the remaining units from step 4.

Make 8.

7. Draw a line on the wrong side of each black 3⅞" half-square triangle as shown. With right sides together, lay a marked triangle on a unit from step 6 as shown. Stitch on the line. Press. Trim away the excess, leaving a ¼" seam allowance. Repeat with the remaining units from step 6.

Make 8.

8. Arrange four striped triangles from step 7 as shown. Sew the triangles into pairs. Press. Sew the pairs together to make a block. Remove the stitching at the seam intersection and press the seam allowances counterclockwise. Repeat to make a total of two blocks.

Make 2.

9. Repeat steps 2–8 with each set of bright and black triangles to make a total of 16 blocks.

Quilt Top Assembly

1. Refer to the quilt assembly diagram on page 68 to lay out the blocks into four rows of four blocks each, balancing the colors as desired. Sew the blocks into rows. To create the "fractured" look, the seams on the sides of the blocks are not intended to meet. If the blocks have been pressed counterclockwise as instructed, the seam allowances at the corners of the blocks should oppose, resulting in accurate corners. Press the seam allowances in opposite directions from row to row. Join the rows to complete the quilt center.

2. Refer to "Plain Borders" on page 12 to measure and cut the black 1¾"-wide first-border strips and sew them to the quilt top, followed by the light green 2"-wide second-border strips, and then the black 1¾"-wide third-border strips. Press the seam allowances toward the newly added border strips after each addition.

3. Using the bias squares you set aside earlier, sew 15 bias squares together to make a side border strip, orienting the bias squares as shown. Repeat to make a total of two border strips. Sew 17 bias squares together to make the top border strip. Repeat to make the bottom border strip.

Side border.
Make 2.

Top/bottom border.
Make 2.

4. Refer to "Pieced Borders" on page 13 and the quilt assembly diagram on page 68 to sew the side borders to the sides of the quilt top, being careful to orient the strips as shown. Press the seam allowances toward the black third border. Sew the top and bottom border strips to the

top and bottom edges of the quilt top. Press the seam allowances toward the black third border.

5. Refer to "Plain Borders" to measure and cut the black 2"-wide fifth-border strips and sew them to the quilt top. Press the seam allowances toward the black border.

6. Referring to steps 3 and 4, use the remaining bias squares to make the pieced sixth-border strips. Make the side border strips with 18 bias squares each and the top and bottom border strips with 20 bias squares each. Sew the borders to the quilt top, again *being careful to orient each strip as shown in the assembly diagram*. Press the seam allowances toward the black fifth border.

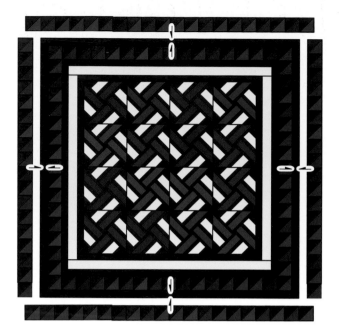

7. Repeat step 5 with the black 3½"-wide seventh-border strips. Press the seam allowances toward the black border.

Quilt assembly

Finishing

1. Layer the quilt top with batting and backing; baste the layers together.

2. Quilt as desired.

3. Bind the quilt edges with the black print 2¼"-wide strips.

MASTER ME QUILTS

Page 70

Page 74

Page 80

Page 87

Stars and Stripes Forever

 Make this patriotic wall banner to honor your favorite service member. Having three veterans in my own family—my husband and two sons—I'm always fond of patriotic quilts.

Finished quilt size: 17½" x 33½"
Finished block size: 8"
Blocks needed: 3

Materials
Yardage is based on 42"-wide fabric.
⅝ yard of dark blue small star print for blocks, outer border, and binding
⅜ yard of white print for blocks and middle border
¼ yard of red print for blocks and inner border
¼ yard or 1 fat quarter of medium blue print for blocks
1 fat quarter of dark blue large star print for block centers
⅔ yard of fabric for backing
20" x 36" piece of batting

Cutting
From the medium blue print, cut:
2 strips, 2½" x 42"; crosscut into 24 squares, 2½" x 2½"

From the white print, cut:
3 strips, 2½" x 42"; crosscut into 24 rectangles, 2½" x 4"
2 strips, 1¾" x 42"

From the red print, cut:
2 strips, 3½" x 42"; crosscut into 12 rectangles, 2½" x 3½"*
2 strips, 1¼" x 42"

From the dark blue small star print, cut:
1 strip, 2½" x 42"; crosscut into 12 squares, 2½" x 2½"
3 strips, 3" x 42"
3 strips, 2¼" x 42"

From the dark blue large star print, fussy cut:
3 squares, 4½" x 4½", centering a star in each square
If your fabric is at least 42", you only need 1 strip.

Block Assembly
Press all seam allowances in the direction of the arrows.

1. Refer to "Striped Rectangles" on page 19 to draw a diagonal line on the wrong side of each medium blue square. Sew marked squares to 12 white rectangles as shown; press, and trim away the excess, leaving a ¼" seam allowance. Set aside the remaining marked blue squares.

Make 12.

2. Draw a diagonal line on the wrong side of each red rectangle. Sew a marked rectangle to each unit from step 1 as shown; press, and trim away as before.

Make 12.

By Donna Lynn Thomas; machine quilted by Pam Goggans

3. Draw a diagonal line on the wrong side of each remaining white rectangle. Sew a marked rectangle on each unit from step 2 as shown; press and trim as before.

Make 12.

4. Draw a diagonal line on the wrong side of each dark blue small star square. Sew a marked square to each unit from step 3 as shown to complete the striped rectangles; press and trim as before.

Make 12.

5. Refer to "Simple Folded Corners" on page 16 to sew a marked medium blue square on the corner of a large star print 4½" square as shown; press, and trim away the excess, leaving a ¼" seam allowance. Repeat on the remaining three corners to make a block center. Repeat to make a total of three block centers.

Make 3.

6. Partially sew a striped rectangle to a block center. Begin at the upper-left corner of the center square and sew the seam halfway across the square. Backstitch and remove the unit

from your machine. Press. Repeat with the remaining block centers.

Make 3.

7. Sew a striped rectangle to the left side of each unit from step 6. Press.

8. Continue to add striped rectangles to each side of the center squares, working counterclockwise. After you have added the last rectangle, complete the first seam to finish the blocks. Press.

 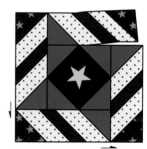

Make 3.

Quilt Top Assembly

1. Refer to the quilt assembly diagram below to sew the blocks together in a vertical row. Press the seam allowances in either direction.

2. Refer to "Plain Borders" on page 12 to sew the red 1¼"-wide inner-border strips to the quilt top, followed by the white 1¾"-wide middle-border strips, and then the dark blue small star print 3"-wide outer-border strips. Press the seam allowances toward the newly added border strip after each addition.

Finishing

1. Layer the quilt top with batting and backing; baste the layers together.

2. Quilt as desired.

3. Bind the quilt edges with the dark blue small star print 2¼"-wide strips.

Quilt assembly

Star Trails

 It was fun adding stripes to this traditional star block to create star "trails." Grading the prints in each stripe from dark to light helps create the effect of cosmic dust trails around the stars. Each of the 13 blocks in this quilt is made from one set of graded prints. Nine are made using the navy blue background print and four are made using the black background print. If you'd like, try a different navy or black background print with each block instead of one consistent background fabric throughout the quilt. Fat quarters work well and you can also use assorted blacks and navy prints for the other border components. The pinwheel border could also easily be replaced with a plain border, but it's a great way to use the trim-away triangles.

Finished quilt size: 75½" x 75½"
Finished block size: 10"
Blocks needed: 13

Materials
Yardage is based on 42"-wide fabric.

3¾ yards of black print for blocks; setting triangles; second, pieced third, fourth, and pieced sixth borders; and binding

2⅛ yards of navy blue print for blocks and pieced sixth border

11" x 16" piece *each* of 13 assorted dark prints for blocks*

10" x 14" piece *each* of 13 assorted light prints for blocks*

9" x 18" piece *each* of 13 assorted medium prints for blocks*

⅞ yard of red print for first and fifth borders

5 yards of fabric for backing

81" x 81" square of batting

*When choosing prints for your blocks, select a color family, and then choose a dark, medium, and light print from that color family.

Cutting

From the navy blue print, cut:

3 strips, 5" x 42"; crosscut into 18 squares, 5" x 5". Cut each square in half diagonally to make 36 half-square triangles.

3 strips, 3" x 42"; crosscut into 36 squares, 3" x 3"

5 strips, 2½" x 42"; crosscut into:
　36 squares, 2½" x 2½"
　36 rectangles, 2½" x 3"

3 strips, 2" x 4"; crosscut into 52 squares, 2" x 2". Cut each square in half diagonally to make 104 half-square triangles.*

4 strips, 6¾" x 42"; crosscut into 22 squares, 6¾" x 6¾"

By Donna Lynn Thomas; machine quilted by Karen Kielmeyer

From *each* of the 13 assorted light prints, cut:

2 squares, 5" x 5" (26 total); cut each square in half diagonally to make 4 half-square triangles (52 total)

4 rectangles, 2½" x 3" (52 total)

From *each* of the 13 assorted dark prints, cut:

5 squares, 2½" x 2½" (65 total)

4 rectangles, 2½" x 3" (52 total)

4 squares, 3½" x 3½" (52 total)

From *each* of the 13 assorted medium prints, cut:

4 squares, 4" x 4" (52 total)

4 rectangles, 2½" x 3" (52 total)

From the black print, cut:

1 strip, 5" x 42"; crosscut into 8 squares, 5" x 5". Cut each square in half diagonally to make 16 half-square triangles.

2 strips, 3" x 42"; crosscut into 16 squares, 3" x 3"

3 strips, 2½" x 42"; crosscut into:

    16 squares, 2½" x 2½"

    16 rectangles, 2½" x 3"

3 strips, 2" x 42"; crosscut into 52 squares, 2" x 2". Cut each square in half diagonally to make 104 half-square triangles.*

4 strips, 6¾" x 42"; crosscut into 22 squares, 6¾" x 6¾"

11 strips, 2¾" x 42"

1 strip, 16" x 42"; crosscut into 2 squares, 16" x 16". Cut each square into quarters diagonally to make 8 side setting triangles.

1 strip, 8½" x 42"; crosscut into 2 squares, 8½" x 8½". Cut each square in half diagonally to make 4 corner setting triangles.

8 strips, 2¼" x 42"

From the red print, cut:

5 strips, 2" x 42"

7 strips, 2½" x 42"

Do not cut these pieces if you're not making the pinwheel border.

Block Assembly

For each block, use light, medium, and dark pieces from the same color family and determine whether you'll use navy blue or black background pieces; use black for four blocks and blue for nine blocks. Press all seam allowances in the direction of the arrows. Reserve all trim-away triangles from each step for the pieced border.

1. Refer to "Striped Rectangles" on page 19 to draw a diagonal line on the wrong side of four background 2½" squares. Sew each marked background square to a light 2½" x 3" rectangle as shown; press, and trim away the excess, leaving a ¼" seam allowance.

    Make 4.

2. Draw a diagonal line on the wrong side of each of the four medium 2½" x 3" rectangles. Sew a marked rectangle to each unit from step 1 as shown; press and trim as before.

    Make 4.

3. In the same fashion, mark, sew, press, and trim a dark 2½" x 3" rectangle to each unit from step 2, followed by a background 2½" x 3" rectangle.

    Make 4.

4. Draw a diagonal line on the wrong side of each of the four dark 2½" squares. Sew a marked square to each unit from step 3 as shown; press and trim as before.

Make 4.

5. Refer to "Add-an-Inch Bias Squares" on page 11 to sew a background 5" half-square triangle to each of the four light half-square triangles along their long edges. Press. Trim the bias squares to 4½".

Make 4.

6. Refer to "Striped Squares" on page 18 to draw a diagonal line on the wrong side of each of the four medium 4" squares. Sew a marked square to the light corner of each bias square from step 5; press and trim as before.

Make 4.

7. In the same fashion, sew a dark 3½" square to each unit from step 6, followed by a background 3" square as shown. Press. Trim away the excess, leaving a ¼" seam allowance.

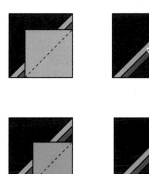

Make 4.

8. Lay out the four striped rectangles, the four striped squares, and the dark 2½" dark square as shown. Sew the patches into rows, aligning diagonal seams. Press. Join the rows to form a block. Press.

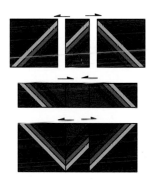 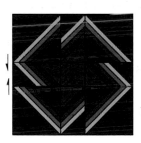

Make 1.

9. Repeat steps 1–8 to make a total of 13 blocks, each from a different color family.

Quilt Top Assembly

1. Lay out the blocks and black side and corner setting triangles in diagonal rows so that the black and blue block backgrounds form a checkerboard. Alternate the direction of the final two outside seams from block to block in the layout. Sew the blocks into diagonal rows. Press the seam allowances in opposite directions from row to row. Join the rows to complete the quilt center.

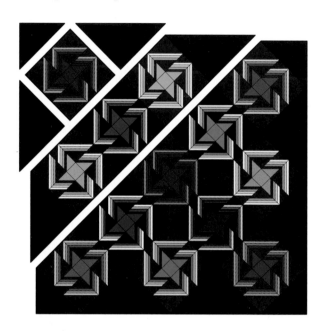

2. Trim the edges of the quilt top ¼" from the block points, squaring the corners at the same time.

3. Refer to "Plain Borders" on page 12 and the quilt assembly diagram on page 79 to measure and cut the red 2"-wide first-border strips and sew them to the quilt top. Press the seam allowances toward the border strips. Repeat to add the black 2¾"-wide second-border strips.

4. You should have a total of 208 black and blue trim-away triangles, along with the 208 cut from the black and blue strips. You should also have 416 trim-away triangles from the light, medium, and dark prints. The triangles must measure no less than 2" along the short edges

in order to work. Refer to "Add-an-Inch Bias Squares" to pair each light, medium, and dark triangle with a black or blue triangle to make 416 bias squares. Press. Trim each bias square to 1½".

Make 416.

5. Randomly sew four different-colored bias squares together to make a pinwheel unit as shown. Press the seam allowances in a clockwise direction, allowing the seam allowances to oppose when the units are sewn together. Remove the stitching at the seam intersection so that the final seam allowances can be pressed in opposite directions. Make 104 units.

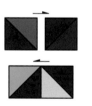

Make 104.

6. Sew the pinwheel units into four border strips of 25 pinwheels each. Refer to "Pieced Borders" on page 13 and the quilt assembly diagram to sew two border strips to the sides of the quilt top. Press the seam allowances toward the black second border. Sew a pinwheel unit to each end of the remaining two border strips. Press the seam allowances toward the end units. Sew these border strips to the top and bottom of the quilt top. Press the seam allowances toward the black second border.

7. Refer to "Plain Borders" to measure and cut the black 2¾"-wide fourth-border strips and sew them to the quilt top, followed by the red 2½"-wide fifth-border strips. Your quilt should measure 63" square at this point.

8. Alternately sew five black and five navy blue 6¾" squares together to make a pieced sixth-border strip. Repeat to make a total of four border strips. Press the seam allowances in either direction. Refer to "Pieced Borders" on page 13 to sew two of these strips to the sides of the quilt top. Press the seam allowances toward the pieced border strips. Sew a black or navy 6¾" square to each end of the two remaining border strips so that the colors alternate. Press the seam allowances toward the center of the border strips. Sew the borders to the top and bottom of the quilt top. Press the seam allowances toward the pieced border.

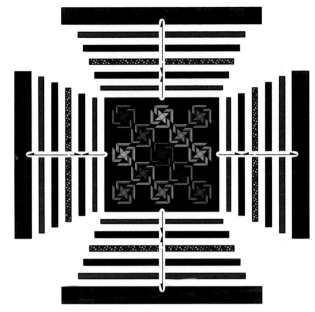

Quilt assembly

Finishing

1. Layer the quilt top with batting and backing; baste the layers together.

2. Quilt as desired.

3. Bind the quilt edges with the black print 2¼"-wide strips.

Color Option

Spring Is Bustin' Out All Over **by Linda Kittle, 75½" x 75½". Apple green and red make for a cheerfully uplifting quilt. Notice that Linda pieced her binding from the various white prints for a fine finishing touch.**

Blackford Blue

Careful use of value provides the gradation of dark to light to dark that connects the blocks to each other, pulling your eye across the quilt. The chain blocks and borders further reinforce the movement with their graded brown values.

Finished quilt size: 64½" x 64½"
Finished block size: 16"
Blocks needed: 4

Materials

Yardage is based on 42"-wide fabric.

1⅞ yards of large-scale dark brown print for blocks, seventh border, and binding

¾ yard of dark blue print for blocks and pieced fifth border

1 yard of medium-dark blue print for blocks and pieced fifth border

1 yard of medium blue print for blocks and pieced fifth border

1½ yards of light blue print for blocks, pieced fifth border, and sixth border

⅓ yard of dark tan print for blocks and fourth border

⅓ yard of medium tan print for blocks and third border

⅓ yard of light tan print for blocks and second border

⅞ yard of cream print for blocks and first border

4¼ yards of fabric for backing

70" x 70" square of batting

Cutting

From the cream print, cut:
4 strips, 2½" x 42"; crosscut 2 of the strips into 32 squares, 2½" x 2½"
2 strips, 4½" x 42"
4 strips, 1½" x 42"

From the dark tan print, cut:
1 strip, 2½" x 42"
4 strips, 1½" x 42"

From the medium tan print, cut:
1 strip, 2½" x 42"
4 strips, 1½" x 42"

From the light tan print, cut:
1 strip, 2½" x 42"
4 strips, 1½" x 42"

From the large-scale dark brown print, cut:
1 strip, 4½" x 42"; crosscut into 4 squares, 4½" x 4½"
2 strips, 2½" x 42"; crosscut into 32 squares, 2½" x 2½"
6 strips, 5½" x 42"
7 strips, 2¼" x 42"

From the dark blue print, cut:
9 strips, 2½" x 42"; crosscut into:
    32 rectangles, 2½" x 3½"
    84 squares, 2½" x 2½"

From the medium-dark blue print, cut:
11 strips, 2½" x 42"; crosscut into 112 rectangles, 2½" x 3½"
1 strip, 3½" x 42"; crosscut into 4 squares, 3½" x 3½"

By Donna Lynn Thomas; machine quilted by Denise Mariano

wrong side of each dark blue 2½" square. With right sides together, lay a marked square on the corner of a medium-dark blue rectangle as shown. Sew on the line. Press. Trim away the excess, leaving a ¼" seam allowance. Repeat to make a total of 40 units.

Make 40.

4. In the same fashion as for the block striped rectangles, mark, sew, press, and trim a medium blue rectangle and then a light blue 2½" square to each unit from step 3 to complete the striped rectangle border units.

Make 40.

5. Repeat steps 3 and 4, positioning the squares and rectangles as shown to make 40 mirror-image striped rectangles.

Make 40.

6. Sew one striped rectangle from step 4 and one from step 5 together along the long edges. Begin stitching at the end where the diagonal seams meet. The seam allowances should be

pressed in opposite directions to create perfect points. Repeat to make a total of 40 rectangle pairs.

Make 40.

7. Refer to "Add-an-Inch Bias Squares" on page 11 to sew a medium blue and light blue 5" half-square triangle together along their long edges to make a bias square. Press. Repeat to make a total of four bias squares. Trim the bias squares to 4½".

Make 4.

8. Draw a diagonal line on the wrong side of each medium-dark blue 3½" square. Sew a marked square to the medium-dark blue corner of each bias square from step 7; press and trim as before.

Make 4.

9. In the same fashion, mark, sew, press, and trim a dark blue 2½" square to the medium-dark blue corner of each unit from step 8 to complete the border corner squares.

Make 4.

10. Sew the rectangle pairs into four strips of 10 units each. Refer to "Pieced Borders" on page 13 and the quilt assembly diagram to sew two pieced border strips to the sides of the quilt top, positioning the dark blue side of the strips toward the quilt center. Press the seam allowances toward the dark tan border.

Make 4.

11. Sew a striped square to each end of the two remaining pieced border strips. Press. Refer to the quilt assembly diagram to sew these border strips to the top and bottom edges of the quilt top. Press the seam allowances toward the dark tan border.

Make 2.

12. Refer to "Plain Borders" to measure and cut the light blue 3½"-wide sixth-border strips and sew them to the quilt top, followed by the dark brown 5½"-wide seventh-border strips. Press the seam allowances toward the newly added border strip after each addition.

Finishing

1. Layer the quilt top with batting and backing; baste the layers together.

2. Quilt as desired.

3. Bind the quilt edges with the dark brown 2¼"-wide strips.

Quilt assembly

Color Option

Blackford's Gradations by Barbara Eikmeier, 64" x 64". Barbara graded her purple prints with remarkable effect. This quilt sparkles and gently moves your eye around the surface.

Warm by the Fire

The single block in this quilt is colored in two ways, with the blocks alternating to create a secondary design. The inner borders are pieced in points to frame the quilt in an unusual fashion. All the warm and cozy cinnamons, browns, and taupes make me think of grabbing a good book, wrapping myself in a quilt, and stretching out on a sofa by a warm fire. The bit of purple adds a spark of cool to a very warm quilt.

Finished quilt size: 78½" x 78½"
Finished block size: 16"
Blocks needed: 5 Block A and 4 Block B

Materials
Yardage is based on 42"-wide fabric.
3⅞ yards of black print for blocks, pieced first and second borders, fourth border, and binding
2⅛ yards of red batik for pieced first and second borders and for third border
1¾ yards of red print for blocks and pieced first border
1⅜ yards of cream print for blocks and pieced first border
¾ yard of tan print for block A
⅝ yard of gray print for block B
½ yard of purple print for blocks
7 yards of fabric for backing
84" x 84" square of batting

Cutting
Sort and label all pieces by color and size. Many sizes are similar, which makes it easy to use the wrong pieces if they aren't labeled.

From the black print, cut:
2 strips, 5" x 42"; crosscut into 12 squares, 5" x 5".
    Cut each square in half diagonally to make 24 half-square triangles.
1 strip, 4½" x 42"; crosscut into 5 squares, 4½" x 4½"
4 strips 3" x 42"; crosscut into 50 squares, 3" x 3".
    Cut each square in half diagonally to make 100 half-square triangles.
18 strips, 2½" x 42"; crosscut into:
    72 squares, 2½" x 2½"
    144 rectangles, 2½" x 3"
5 strips, 1½" x 42"; crosscut into:
    16 rectangles, 1½" x 8½"
    28 squares, 1½" x 1½"
8 strips, 3½" x 42"
9 strips, 2¼" x 42"

From the tan print, cut:
9 strips, 2½" x 42"; crosscut into:
    20 rectangles, 2½" x 4½"
    100 squares, 2½" x 2½"

From the red print, cut:
16 strips, 2½" x 42"; crosscut into:
    64 squares, 2½" x 2½"
    144 rectangles, 2½" x 3"
3 strips, 3" x 42"; crosscut into 32 squares, 3" x 3".
    Cut each square in half diagonally to make 64 half-square triangles.
1 strip, 4½" x 42"; crosscut into 4 squares, 4½" x 4½"
2 strips, 1½" x 4"; crosscut into 36 squares, 1½" x 1½"

From the gray print, cut:

7 strips, 2½" x 42"; crosscut into:

    16 rectangles, 2½" x 4½"

    80 squares, 2½" x 2½"

From the cream print, cut:

2 strips, 5" x 42"; crosscut into 12 squares, 5" x 5".
    Cut each square in half diagonally to make 24
    half-square triangles.

7 strips, 3" x 42"; crosscut into 82 squares, 3" x 3".
    Cut each square in half diagonally to make 164
    half-square triangles.

7 strips, 2½" x 42"; crosscut into 100 squares,
    2½" x 2½"

From the purple print, cut:

5 strips, 2½" x 42"; crosscut into 72 squares,
    2½" x 2½"

From the red batik, cut:

3 strips, 3½" x 42"; crosscut into 24 squares,
    3½" x 3½"

3 strips, 1½" x 42"; crosscut into 12 rectangles,
    1½" x 8½"

7 strips, 7½" x 42"

Block Assembly

Press all seam allowances in the direction of the
arrows.

1. Draw a diagonal line on the wrong side of 40
   black 2½" squares. Sew a marked square to
   each tan 2½" x 4½" rectangle as shown; press,
   and trim away the excess, leaving a ¼" seam
   allowance. Repeat on the opposite side of each
   rectangle to make 20 flying-geese units.

Make 20.

2. Lay out four flying-geese units, one black 4½"
   square, and four tan 2½" squares as shown. Sew
   the pieces into rows. Press. Join the rows to
   make a block. Press. Repeat to make a total of
   five black star units.

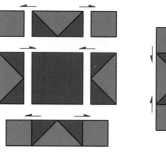 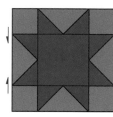

Make 5.

3. Repeat steps 1 and 2 using 32 red 2½" squares,
   16 gray 2½" x 4½" rectangles, four red 4½"
   squares, and 16 gray 2½" squares to make four
   red star units.

Make 4.

4. Refer to "Striped Rectangles" on page 19 to
   draw a diagonal line on the wrong side of
   36 cream 2½" squares and 36 red 2½" x 3"
   rectangles. Sew each of the cream squares to
   a black 2½" x 3" rectangle as shown; press and
   trim as before. In the same fashion, sew a red
   2½" x 3" rectangle to each unit; press and trim.

Make 36.

Donna Lynn Thomas; machine quilted by Sandy Gore

3. Referring to "Add-an-Inch Bias Squares," sew a black 5" half-square triangle to a cream 5" half-square triangle along the long edge. Repeat to make a total of 24 bias squares. Press the seam allowances of 12 bias squares toward the black and the remaining 12 toward the cream. Trim the bias squares to 4½".

Make 12.   Make 12.

4. Draw a diagonal line on the wrong side of each red batik 3½" square. Sew a marked square to the black corner of each bias square from step 3; press and trim.

Make 24.

5. Sew the striped squares from step 4 into pairs, being careful to orient them so that the seam allowances are pressed as shown.

6. Sew the units from steps 2 and 5 into four pieced borders as shown. Do not press the seam allowances.

Side border.
Make 2.

Top/bottom border.
Make 2.

7. Referring to "Pieced Borders" on page 13, sew the side pieced border strips to the sides of the quilt top, pressing the seam allowances on the border strips so that they oppose the seam allowances of the quilt center. Press the seam allowance toward the pieced border. Join the top and bottom pieced border strips to the top and bottom edges of the quilt top in the same manner.

8. Draw a diagonal line on the wrong side of 24 black 1½" squares. Sew a marked square to the end of a red batik 1½" x 8½" rectangle as shown; press, and trim, leaving a ¼" seam allowance. Repeat on the opposite corner of each rectangle to make 12 pieced border strips.

Make 12.

9. For the second border, alternately join three pieced border strips from step 8 and four black 1½" x 8½" rectangles as shown. Repeat to make a total of four border strips.

10. Sew the side pieced border strips to the quilt top. Press the seam allowances toward the newly added border strips. Add a black 1½" square to the ends of the two remaining pieced border strips. Press the seam allowances away from the squares. Sew the border strips to the top and bottom edges of the quilt top. Press.

11. For the third border, refer to "Plain Borders" on page 12 to measure, cut, and sew the red batik 7½"-wide strips to the quilt top. For the fourth border, repeat with the black 3½"-wide strips.

Finishing

1. Layer the quilt top with batting and backing; baste the layers together.

2. Quilt as desired.

3. Bind the quilt edges with the black 2¼"-wide strips.

Quilt assembly

Pinwheel Chain Bonus Block

 The Pinwheel Chain block is the perfect block for using up all those leftover triangles trimmed away from your quilt tops. If you wish to augment your triangle trim-away collection, cut 2" squares of assorted dark and light prints in half diagonally to make half-square triangles. Cut as many as you need for the number of blocks you want to make. Make as many blocks as you wish from the quilt leftovers until you have enough to make a quilt of any size.

Finished block size: 10"

Materials (for 1 block)

36 dark trim-away triangles no smaller than 2" on both short edges

36 light trim-away triangles no smaller than 2" on both short edges

16 assorted light squares, 2½" x 2½"

Block Assembly

Press all seam allowances in the direction of the arrows.

1. Refer to steps 4 and 5 of "Add-an-Inch Bias Squares" on page 11 to sew each light triangle to a dark triangle along their long edges to make 36 bias squares. It's OK if they're ragged

in appearance. Press the seam allowances toward the dark fabric. Trim each bias square to 1½".

Make 36.

2. Sew four bias squares together to make a pinwheel unit. Press, removing the stitching at the seam intersection on the final seam so that the seam allowances can be pressed counterclockwise. Repeat to make a total of nine units.

Make 9.

3. Lay out the pinwheel units and the light 2½" squares as shown. Sew the pieces into rows. Press. Join the rows to complete the block. Press.

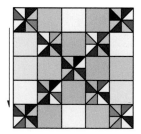 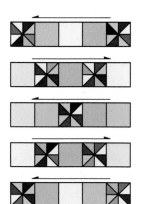

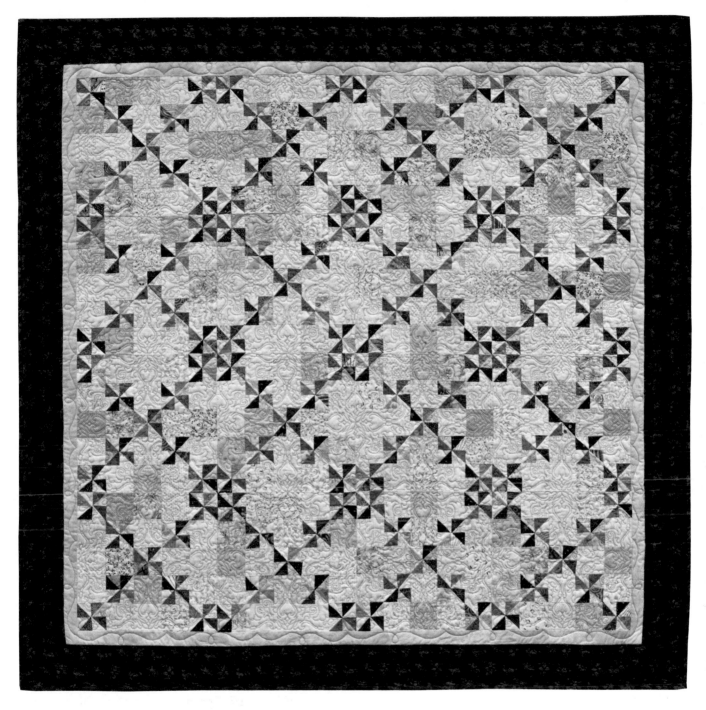

Alice's Jewels by Alice Zeman, 48" x 48"; machine quilted by Denise Mariano.

This beautiful quilt was constructed entirely using "trim-aways" from the quilts I made for this book.
Alice works completely from donated fabrics. I sent her the box of leftovers and the pattern, and this was
the result. It truly is Alice's jewel, and I can't wait to make one of my own.

About the Author

Donna has been sewing since the age of four and quilting since 1975. She began teaching in 1981, and since 1988 she has been a National Quilting Association certified teacher for basic quiltmaking (NQACT). While an Army wife, she lived in Germany for four years and taught at a German shop and various guilds throughout the country. Having recently settled back in Kansas for good, Donna still teaches nationally and internationally. The author of many previous quilting titles with Martingale & Company, she has also contributed articles on various quilt-related subjects to numerous publications over the years.

Her greatest joy is her two sons, Joe and Pete, and lovely daughters-in-law, Katie and Nikki. Donna and her husband, Terry, provide accommodations and staff assistance to their three cats, Max, Jack, and Skittles, and a kiddie pool and ear scratches to one sunny golden retriever, Brandy. All the quilts in her house are lovingly pre-furred.

Jack, exhausted from supervising quilt photography, diligently pre-furs some quilts. Photograph by Katie Lynn Thomas.

There's More Online!